6427

FOLLOW ME!

MALCOLM SMITH FOLLOW ME!

THE APPRENTICING OF DISCIPLES

Logos International
Plainfield, New Jersey

FOLLOW ME!

I

The light changed as I pulled away from the curb and headed for home, where Jean and the girls would be asleep. The rain had stopped, and a dismal mist hung in the night over the streets, deserted now but for an occasional drunk and a few Puerto Rican boys throwing firecrackers down the block. To the left of me, the church was a great black hulk silhouetted against the glow of millions of lights from the streets of New York below.

The red light seemed interminable. I peered at it through a windshield covered with a greasy film that the wipers dragged monotonously behind them. Finally the light turned green, and I edged out into Fourth Avenue. In my rear view mirror, I could see a flashing red light rapidly approaching. The wail of a siren came closer echoing down the deserted canyons, and a police car, followed by an ambulance, flashed by showering my windshield with a fresh coat of sludge.

Yawning deeply, I pulled out behind them, just in time to catch the next red light. Even at two thirty in the morning,

1

Brooklyn was stop-and-go driving. I opened the window to wake up with the icy cold of the December night. No, it was January by two and a half hours! We had gathered in Salem Tabernacle in December 1971 and dispersed in January 1972.

As New Year's Eve gatherings went, this one had been glorious. The meal we had shared early in the evening, followed by an hour or so of testimonies by all those who had come to know Christ in the last year, and the communion service, just before midnight, had made the evening the crown to the most unusual year of my life.

A flow of the Holy Spirit that had begun within me a year before that had completely changed me and my life. It had then spread to the neighborhood homes of my congregation in the form of home Bible studies. These home meetings in turn had been the birthplace of a growing number who were to find their spiritual home in the church that met in the Salem Gospel Tabernacle on the corner of Fourth Avenue and 54th Street in Brooklyn, where I was the pastor.

But one incident that night seemed to stand out from all the others. Among the many who attended our meal was a group of fellows and girls in blue jeans and peasant dresses. For our traditionally Norwegian congregation this was something new. In recent months there had been great grace over us all, as they saw the Norwegian image replaced by the influx of families of Italian, Chinese, Jewish and Puerto Rican descent. But until tonight, everyone had been dressed traditionally. I smiled as I remembered the look some of the older church members had given to the youths, and then praised God for the warm welcome they gave them, in spite of what they may have thought of their dress. I dismissed the incident and drove on up Fourth Avenue.

But the incident wouldn't be dismissed. Those young people had been a happy, uninhibited group. They laughed aloud at anything that was slightly humorous—to the consternation of some who never so much as smiled in church.

Odd Titland, one of our deacons, had embraced the boys and introduced them to the younger members of our congregation. One of the new boys, a tall, lean fellow with long blond hair and a big smile on his face, introduced himself as Steve. He had brought the others. There was Ray Ciervo, dark with long black hair, and Lee, a laughing girl in a long dress with hair down to her waist. Again I shook off the memory, thanking God for the new people He was sending to us.

What would this new year hold? I then remembered how it was this same time last year, and tasted again the fear and expectancy I had when I began to walk on the water of a new experience. But on this first day of 1972, I looked forward with uninhibited excitement to whatever the Spirit had in store.

"Where are we going this year, Lord?" I asked aloud, above the hissing of my tires on the wet pavement. It was as if a curtain was raised in my mind. *Go, therefore, and make disciples of all the nations, baptizing them in the name of the Father and the Son and the Holy Spirit, teaching them to observe all that I commanded you; and lo, I am with you always, even to the end of the age.* The words Matthew had recorded came vividly before me. They were as fresh from the lips of the glorified Lord Jesus as the day He first spoke them. At that moment the car seemed so charged with a sense of His presence that I welcomed the red light up ahead. I was awed. The light changed to green, but I sat unwilling to proceed. It was some minutes later that the presence lifted and I slowly pulled away. The words seemed suspended in the night like

3

the mist that hung on the streets of the city outside. Inside, I trembled with anticipation going over them again and again, *all nations . . . make disciples . . .* teach them all things I have taught you.

I imagined the prospect of missionary work all over the world. Six months before I had gone to West Africa, and had spent hours sharing with the native leaders in Liberia all that the Spirit had so recently shown me. Since then, I had longed to return to the mission field and share with other national leaders. In the Christmas mail had been a scrawled note from a native pastor, "We beg you pa Smith to come and teach us plenty too much again." It all fit! I could hardly wait to see how the Holy Spirit would work out my going to all nations.

Abruptly, I realized that the excitement I was now experiencing was no longer that deep, abiding joy that comes from insight in the Spirit. This was a shallow, emotional thing, self-exalting and there was the stench of death about it. I stopped my racing mind and returned quietly to the words of Scripture. Again I spoke aloud: "What does it mean, Lord?" It was peaceful now in the car, no distraction apart from the hum of the engine and the hiss of the car sliding along the wet road. Even so, the answer did not come right away.

Maybe I should shelve the text, I thought, a little impatiently. I certainly couldn't forget it, and He would in the next months explain what it meant in my life. Fourth Avenue fell behind me. Garbage cans piled high with discarded Christmas junk sprawled soggily outside grim, dark apartments that housed hundreds of Puerto Ricans and Colombians. The Brooklyn-Queens Expressway loomed up ahead and then was behind me. And with it, the neighborhood changed from Spanish-speaking to Italian.

The fact that Brooklyn was divided into clearly discernible ethnic sections was something I had never ceased to marvel at. Here were the Italians, behind me the Colombians, the Puerto Ricans, and a few blocks away, Eighth Avenue was all Norwegian and Swedish. Beyond them, Orthodox Russian Jews, dressed in fur hats and black coats lived in a world all their own. It was like driving through one country after another, without need of a passport or having to stop at the border. Almost every nation under the sun must be represented within a thirty-mile radius of this spot.

Then it hit me. "My Lord! All nations—*right here!*" I shouted the words aloud. An excitement, born of the Spirit, rose within me.

I was able to find a parking place a couple of blocks from our apartment and started walking home. I was no longer the least bit tired. The low moan of fog horns from the Hudson River a few blocks away punctuated the silence and suited my mood perfectly. I drew my coat closer around me. *Make disciples of all the nations.* What did I know of making disciples? I realized vaguely that the word meant something a little more than being a believer. But there was something in the past, something that would show what it was. I groped back to an incident that had happened in England, just before we had come to the United States.

Jean and I were living in Loughborough in Leicestershire, a sleepy little town in the center of England. We conducted missions and called people to commit themselves to Christ. These commitments were carefully recorded and filed. At the same time, we had kept up a casual, friendly fellowship with another evangelist, Rob Smith, who had moved onto the local campus to evangelize the students. At the end of his first year in the town, he invited us over for dinner.

The conversation drifted to what we had been doing in evangelism. Then, quite suddenly, Rob looked at me and

5

said, "How many disciples have you made this year?" I glowed inside at the question. With a poor attempt at humility, I told him of the thousand and some cards we had on file of those who had committed themselves to Christ. He looked at me sternly and said, "How many are *discipled?* How many of those are now discipling others?"

I felt weak in my stomach. I knew I was out of my depth and was ashamed to show my ignorance. Rob saw my embarrassment and gently said, "Let me put it this way, how many of those have come to maturity, and have in turn won another and are presently engaged in bringing that one to maturity?"

And now the awful truth that I had always known, came into the open. "Rob," I could barely get the words out, "I don't know if twenty-five per cent have kept up with their commitment, and probably only one in a hundred is the kind of person you describe. If I knew how to handle that. . . ." My voice trailed away.

Rob waited a moment, then spoke quietly, "We moved into this town about the same time. While you gave the Word to the masses, I asked the Lord to give me one individual. He gave me one, and then another and another until there were ten in all. We sat together, and I gave my life to them. Everything the Lord had ever taught me, I taught them." He paused, and then said, "Now they are doing the same." I was speechless at the simplicity and sense of it. "Malcolm," Rob concluded, "God has called you to the masses, no doubt. But you should aim at making disciples *while* you address them."

The words sank in and were filed in some remote corner of my brain. Now they came rushing back. The words of Jesus were so fresh that they still seemed to ring in the sound of my own footsteps. I realized that, in a sense, the discipling had already begun to happen, but there had to be

6

more to it than what I had seen. I remembered the boys in blue jeans. If fellows like that could be taught in a year, or maybe two, what it had taken me twenty years to learn. . . . If they could be discipled to Jesus as He had discipled the twelve—my heart quickened at the thought. No longer a stream of backsliders going forward at every altar call to get right with God. No longer failures, but mature men of God who knew what they believed, who understood their experience with God and whose lives were daily being molded more after the life of Jesus.

A fellow minister had poured out his heart to me just before the Christmas vacation. "Malcolm, all I do is convince Christians they ought to keep on being Christians—isn't there a better way?" I had said a lot on that occasion, but surely *this* was the answer that he—and I—had been seeking. As I walked up the steps of our duplex apartment and inserted the key in the lock, I realized my hand was trembling.

Sleep wouldn't come that night. Around and around went the words, *All nations . . . go and make disciples . . . street kids like Steve and Ray . . . not just believers, but mature men of God who would disciple others . . . all nations. . . .*

II

It was March now. Outside the local diner an old yellowed newspaper tossed and whirled in the chill wind. Floyd, my assistant pastor, straddled the brown-topped stool beside me and ordered some coffee.

"What's new?" I asked him.

"We had a meeting at Peter and Ruth's last night—had a long talk with Ray afterward." I thought of the dark boy with the long black hair, who wanted to follow Christ with a passion that drove him to every service of the church. "He wants to go to Bible school," Floyd said, sipping at the steaming mug.

"Bible school?" I exclaimed, scalding my tongue. Somehow, Ray's long hair and blue jeans didn't fit into any Bible school I knew. I couldn't see him accepting the usual dress codes and traditions that were common to them all. This boy had new life, and deep inside I was afraid lest he should lose it for a lot of theological words in a place of formal education. "What did you tell him?" I asked in a quieter tone.

8

"I let him do most of the talking, actually. But I believe he really has a call. Do you know he is working like a slave in that cab, and saving every penny so he can support himself when he goes? I told him we'd pray about it and talk it over with the elders."

A phrase that I had put out of mind for weeks now flickered at the edge of my consciousness—*make disciples.* Here was one of the young people that had first challenged me—and now he was asking for teaching. Where *could* we send a boy like that?

My mind drifted to the home meetings we had recently been holding throughout this neighborhood. Eager young people—long-haired fellows like Ray, girls in peasant dresses or jeans like Lee—had pressed into apartments and enthusiastically responded to the proclaiming of the Gospel and the testimonies of new converts. Ray had shared his testimony at least a dozen times. Each time I marveled at the grace of God that was in the telling. You could almost see it happening. As we drank our coffee in thoughtful silence, I seemed to experience it again.

A group of hippies, four boys and a girl, slept in the cool stillness of the early morning. Above them, the clear sky gradually filled with red glory. The sun rose above the massive rock cliffs that surrounded them and filtered down through the fir trees in a lacy veil of warm gold.

Slowly, Ray opened his eyes and closed them again. His head was throbbing and fuddled. He waited, wincing, as the world gradually came into focus. They were high in the Sierra Nevadas in Yosemite National Park. The day before, they had come upon this spot which a sign had said was Tuolumne Meadows.

He ran his hand through the thick black matted hair around his neck. The sound of birds outside made him feel strangely good. Somewhere he heard a stream splashing and gurgling. Crawling out of his sleeping bag he made his way over the bodies of his still sleeping companions. There was Freddy, a lifetime friend, whom he had grown up with in Brooklyn. Then there was Ron, Joe and Leonora, who had become friends during the last few months.

They had been on the road for weeks, on a zigzag path across country from Brooklyn to California. For the past year he had slept in parks and empty apartment houses; his life had been a continual drug trip, financed by unemployment checks and money made from black-marketing in Vietnam. When money got short, they had stolen food from supermarket delivery vans. At the beginning of the warm weather, bored and restless, they had set out for California.

Ray gazed at the rugged majesty of the sun-swept mountains, and again something stirred inside him. To his reading of eastern philosophy he had added the story of the North American Indian and his near destruction by the white man. The calculated lies told by the whites to the red man, followed by brutal senseless murder in the name of civilization enraged him. As if that were not enough, the sadistic murders were glorified on television, and the white murderers idolized.

He had begun to look on himself as non-white. Mentally, he had disassociated himself from the white man who seemed to have done little but wipe out any culture that had a grasp of what civilized behavior really was—the simple, honest Indian, the small, poverty-stricken Vietnamese. This was what man was made for, the woods and mountains and simple living. A few days before they had passed through a city and he had stared up at a vast apartment complex. At the thought of sixty thousand people living piled on top of each other like rats in a cage, he had become physically nauseated.

Deciding not to wake the others, he stepped into a clearing and looked around him. A sparkling river moved swiftly toward a falls, throwing shafts of light in all directions. White slabs of rock soared heavenward in front of him, smooth as if planed and chiseled by some giant hand. He came to the falls where the river plunged into a ravine far below and crept out on a span of rock, till he was standing directly above the falls. Behind him, the peaks of the Sierra Nevadas seemed almost touchable. He felt like a gnat in a giant's world. He gasped and found himself saying, "Someone *made* all of this."

Incidents, scenes, reactions from the forgotten past all began to fall together. It was as if a hand had spanned the years, taken meaningless pieces of a jigsaw puzzle and begun to rapidly form a picture.

He remembered a forest fire that he had fought while he was in Vietnam. A wall of fire was closing in, in front and at the side, forcing the firefighters back into the ammunition dump. The heat was unbelievable; he could hardly bear to take it into his lungs. He half expected to hear the first explosions, ignited by the heat alone. Flaming branches crashed down around him. Smoke filled his lungs and choked him. He realized it was only a matter of seconds before he and the desperate soldiers on either side of him would be blown to a million pieces.

He had never thought much about God before, but now, as a shower of sparks seared his flesh and started his clothes smoldering, he wanted to pray. He couldn't get any words out, the air was too hot to take in. But the prayer formed distinctly in his mind and he knew he was communicating with Someone. *God, I don't want to die.*

A moment later, incredibly, the wind changed, blowing the blaze away from them and the ammunition dump. Tears had stuck his singed eyelashes together.

11

The God who had saved him that morning had made all of this. He who had controlled the wind, had carved out these ravines and created the Sierra Nevadas. *Who are you?* he asked aloud, and not for the first time. He had started asking that question in Vietnam right after the fire. Another GI had given one answer by introducing Ray to Buddha, and the road to Nirvana. It had led to denying his body sleep and food, and to long periods of meditation. In order to endure it, he had begun to take increasing amounts of opium. Seeking to meditate, he had lain for hours on the 110° sand, smoking the pipe. He had turned, still empty and searching, to eastern philosophies.

Ray had come back to Brooklyn a hippie. He lived for months off the profit he had made selling black-market beer, cigarettes, and whiskey in Saigon. He realized that the journey he and his friends were now on was part of that search—a search for reality and meaning, for the name of the God who had become enmeshed in the fabric of his life. The memories continued to rush up from deep within, pent-up cries for God—whoever He or It was. The horizon-to-horizon splendor of His creation had brought it all together.

Balanced precariously above the falls, Ray raised his hands as if to embrace and inhale it all. He cried aloud, *God, whoever You are, that made all of this, I want to know You.*

The echo of his cry came back to him—*Know you . . . Know you. . .* Then all was silent, save for the water rushing beneath the rock on which he stood and the sound of the falls below.

They reached Los Angeles a few days later. It was as boring as Brooklyn. As long as they were in motion they didn't have to face the stark emptiness of their lives. It was hidden behind the next place they were heading for on the road. Motion itself with its vague unspecified promise became the goal. It didn't matter *where* they were going as long as they were *going*. And so the van headed back east.

In Denver they stopped and sprawled out on the grass. Ray sat cross-legged, and strummed on a guitar. He heard conversation behind him, and looking over his shoulder saw two fellows dressed like himself earnestly engaged in conversation with his friends. He continued to strum, listening to what they had to say.

Their words made something leap inside of him. They spoke of God as if they knew Him personally. In fact, they said He had come in the person of Jesus, to die for sinners. Ray had heard of Jesus and of His death, but had never dreamed that he was in some way benefited by it, as the fellow with the guitar was saying.

He listened, drinking in the words. God loved him, just as he was, guilty, empty and messed-up. He loved him with the kind of love that didn't demand return but kept on loving in spite of being rejected. Love that had taken the place of the messed-up sinner and took to Himself the punishment due. With a transparent sincerity, the young man announced that Jesus was alive and Lord, and would come into anyone's life who would ask Him.

To Ray, it was water in an arid desert, and he wanted very badly to hear more. When the young hippie evangelists invited Ray and his friends back to their base of operation in the city, they all enthusiastically accepted. Walking through the park, the two boys introduced themselves as "Parable" and "Oboth," members of a rapidly growing movement called the Children of God. Upon accepting Christ as the new master of their lives, they had renounced the world and all family ties, adopted new names taken from the Bible, and had gone to live in a mountain commune.

The idea of renouncing the world added fuel to the fire that had begun to burn inside of Ray. Civilization had lost

13

all attraction for him, and he was almost ready to leave it for the simplicity he had found in the mountains. As they sat on the floor of the garden apartment that night, Parable told them of their commune at Waldon, high up in the Rocky Mountains. By morning Ray was ready to kneel and pray with Oboth, asking Christ to become his Savior and rescue him from the evil of the world.

Ray and Leonora had prayed while their other friends mocked them. In praying they had found a reason for living. With a new-born enthusiasm they piled into their van to return to New York City. Oboth stood at the driver's window. "You know, you will never make it alone; you must flee the world system. Going back to the city will destroy you." But they had already talked about going to the commune and decided not to. Nonetheless, they accepted directions should they ever change their minds. They drove nonstop and came off the Belt Parkway in the Flatbush section of Brooklyn thirty-three hours later.

For the next few days, Ray sat in doorways with old buddies, urging them to repent and flee the city, the great whore, and live with God in the mountains. No one was impressed. Finally one suggested, "If it's so great, why aren't *you* there?"

That set Ray to thinking: Why, indeed, weren't they there? The temptations of the city were too strong to maintain any kind of Jesus walk. Ray discussed it with Lee, and a new recruit named Stephen, and decided to return to Colorado and find the commune at Waldon. Once more they turned west, this time without the van. After days of hitchhiking with heavy packs, they arrived, footsore, blistered and weary to exhaustion. And they entered into a nightmare.

It seemed to Ray as if they were being processed into jail. Everything except what they needed to wear, to wash with, and to sleep in was taken away, including money, jewelry and personal possessions. A list of rules informed them of rising time, meal times and a list of things they were not allowed to do, which amounted to just about everything Ray had spent all his life doing. He followed Stephen down a narrow passage to the men's wing of the rough-hewn dormitory where there were beds with no mattresses, just bare springs. In a silence, they spread out their sleeping bags. So this was heaven on earth! There was a heaviness about the place, a sense of despondency that filled Ray with foreboding.

The night of their arrival there was a party with singing, dancing, and worship. After a restless night on the bare springs that dug through the sleeping bags, they were awakened at seven. A meager breakfast at eight was followed by a large group prayer meeting. The group split up into smaller groups for Bible study. After a hurried lunch the morning program was repeated, the day finishing with a large group meeting at night.

The days were filled with a harsh application of the rules. It was harder than boot camp; nothing seemed to make any sense. At least in boot camp you could usually see a reason for what was being done.

The two boys stuck it out for a week. Each night they tried to convince each other that tomorrow had to be better. But each day was worse. At the end of the week they could take it no longer. They informed the elders that they were leaving. The elders begged, persuaded, and threatened them for two hours. But Ray and Stephen were adamant; they were leaving.

Solemnly, one of the elders told them that they were choosing to return to the embrace of the whore. They were selling out on God . . . "In fact," he intoned, weighing his words, "you are Judas betraying Christ." They walked in silence down the rutted track when a shout from behind stopped them. "Hey, wait for me!" It was Lee.

It was a silent journey. Each one heard that parting malediction and was ashamed to look at the others. *You are a Judas.* And as the skyline of New York City finally loomed ahead, Ray heard again the words, *into the embrace of the whore.*

Their shame at having become apostates led them to split up. Ray was left alone with his guilt, yet held by a quiet confidence that the Bible held the answer. Driven by guilt, he plunged into a cycle of turning on, stealing, finding heroin pushers, and the nightmare in between. But each night Ray continued the habit of reading his Bible. Sometimes he would be so high that he could not concentrate, but he read it faithfully.

Living on the streets, Ray was delighted when he got an invitation to visit with Ann-Marie and Louis. Ann-Marie was Lee's sister. Louis had been in Vietnam at the same time as Ray, and was good for an evening's conversation.

Finally the subject turned to the past few months. "What happened in Colorado?" asked Louis. "Lee told us a little, but the other guys just wouldn't talk. You got mixed up with a bunch of Jesus freaks, didn't you? What *do* they believe?"

Ray leaned back and took a long drag on his cigarette. The events of the last months were all too unreal; they came to mind in pictures out of sequence, like a slide show in which all the slides were jumbled in the wrong order. But one thing he did know; what he had heard Parable say at the park in Denver was truth, no matter what followed. He did not feel right about what he had seen in the commune. Yet he lived under the bitter guilt of having left them. Then in response to Louis' specific question, he began to explain the good news of a God who loved and had come in the person of Jesus. It was near midnight when he heard himself say,

16

"Louis, Jesus is alive. If you would let Him in, Life will live inside of you."

He was sleeping at his parents' home that night and he walked through the deserted streets to the house. He had sniffed heroin during the evening, and felt the disgust he had had when talking of Christ while being high. If he could have climbed out of his body he would happily have done so. Later, he lay on his bed and read Romans 10. His eyes moved to verses 9 and 10.

> . . . if you confess with your mouth Jesus as Lord and believe in your heart that God raised Him from the dead, you shall be saved; for with the heart man believes resulting in righteousness, and with the mouth he confesses, resulting in salvation.

He rolled over on his back, his mind reeling. His guilt and personal sin seemed to oppress the atmosphere of the room. And now, darkness as a personal entity seemed to have entered the room; demons had come to receive him. Ray felt his skin tighten all over his body. He knew that if he was damned in hell that night, he would be getting exactly what he deserved.

Whosoever shall call on the name of the Lord shall be saved—the words penetrated the confusion of darkness, and he fell to his knees. He saw himself as a sinner in desperate need—something he had never seen before—and he begged Christ to come and be his Lord. He had seen the world was a mess before, but he had always seen himself as righteous and better than the rest. Now he knew otherwise, and asked God to have mercy on him, a sinner. A peace came over him then and he fell into a dreamless sleep.

He awoke in the morning, and threw his clothes on. He knew he needed drugs. But a voice rose from within him,

17

distinct and clearer than his own thoughts, *No, we don't.* Stunned, he sat back on the bed as the events of the previous night came rushing back. He had asked God to cleanse him, and for Christ to take over as Lord. And now *He was there,* ordering him from within to a new way of life.

The next days were not the easiest. He stayed in his room, alone, reading his Bible, as his body threw off its dependency on drugs. After four days, he felt new life in his veins. He was on his way to a new life.

He now *knew* the God who had saved him from fire—who had sculptured the Sierra Nevadas—he *knew* Him in Jesus Christ! How he ached for the mountains—to be away from Babylon, to live with God! He could do it now, he was sure, but his thoughts died away, as the One within said clearly, *We are staying in the city.* And he knew that he would have to live this Jesus life *in* the world without being a part *of* the world.

He was so excited with the sense of the Good News, that he hurried to the streets and his old haunts to find his friends. They were just about to shoot up, as Ray joined them and began witnessing to them of what Christ had done in him. No one seemed to be listening, as they continued their preparations. Finally one of the youths nodded to himself and, smiling knowingly, extended some of the white powder to Ray on the tip of a knife. "Here, old buddy, have some on me. Go ahead, just this once for old time's sake." In that moment Ray knew he was free. He didn't want it, and he didn't need it. He did not need a commune and a strait jacket of regulations to enable him to maintain a semblance of spiritual life. His life came from within his spirit, where Christ had come to live.

He started to work. He had never wanted to work within a society he had lost faith in; he did not understand what was now going on inside of him; all he knew was that he now had

18

to earn a living and support himself. His father owned a yellow cab, and Ray began to drive it around Brooklyn. To his amazement he enjoyed it immensely. The Lord was riding with him and each fare was a fresh opportunity to share what had happened to him. Most of the fares seemed touched and a few were deeply moved. Days sailed into weeks for Ray as the consciousness that Jesus was in him grew.

It was Christmas and the parties began. Ray was asked but he felt a strange loneliness as he went. He could no longer relate to what these people called life. It was at such a party in a large house in the Flatbush section that he saw Steve. Ray had known Steve briefly after returning from Vietnam and then Steve had disappeared from the scene heading west to California six months before Ray had gone himself. As they sat down to talk, Ray sensed something very different about the tall smiling blond. Neither remembers who introduced the subject, but they soon found themselves trying to witness to each other of the saving power of Jesus Christ in their lives.

Steve had come to Christ when his drug supplier had had a miraculous conversion. Now he radiated joy. "Where do you go to church?" he asked.

"Church?" Ray exclaimed. "None of the churches around here believe this. The truth is, I haven't been inside one since I can remember."

Steve pulled a grimy piece of paper from a billfold, with a phone number scrawled on it. It was a church in Manhattan. "My elder in California gave it to me before I left," he explained. "I've only been in town a few hours and haven't had time to call. Why don't we call now? We've got to find a place to fellowship." As he moved through the crowded room to telephone, Ray murmured, "What's fellowship?"

Steve found the young woman's voice on the other end of

19

the line friendly enough, but not too helpful. It was the Christmas vacation period—"We don't have any meetings until after the New Year."

Steve muttered mildly under his breath. "We wanted to have some fellowship on New Year's Eve."

"Sorry, we just close up at this time of year." She paused, and then suddenly, "I'll tell you what; there's a church in Brooklyn that has a service on New Year's Eve. It's Salem Gospel Tabernacle on Fourth Avenue and 54th. I'm sure you would be welcome there."

Steve came back to Ray. "Guess what? We're going to Salem Tabernacle on New Year's Eve."

"Aren't you going to finish your coffee? Here, let me heat it up for you." Dottie's motherly voice brought me back to Fifth Avenue, bemusedly thanking God for leading Steve and Ray to us on New Year's Eve. Now they were asking for Bible school. Where do we go from here, Lord?

I joined Floyd who had already gone outside. The freezing wind bit into us as we walked down 54th Street.

III

My uneasiness of spirit that made me ask Ray to hold off for a while in his decision to go to Bible school was based on more than his long hair and leather-thonged sandals. Not that I have anything against Bible schools, per se. On the contrary, in the past I had proudly sent a number of boys to Bible school from the churches where I had been the pastor.

It was that word *disciple* that made me uneasy. Ever since the night when the Holy Spirit had dropped that word into my heart, I had studied it thoroughly. My thinking had still not crystallized, but a lot of ends were beginning to be braided together. The overall message that I saw emerging from the early church was that Christianity was a practicing religion, one that would not allow me the luxury of being a professional student, any more than it would allow other people to live it for me. Any truth that I grasped must be worked out in my life.

The Pharisees were religious students. They consumed the old covenant Law and thrived on it. They could quote it verbatim, interpret it and explain its fine points. They could do anything except live it! They assumed that to be able to grasp truth intellectually was to be accepted by the God of truth.

Jesus rejected their assumption. He called them hypocrites, or "play actors"—"those who wear a mask." They masked who they were with volumes of religious expertise. But however elaborate, their mask was incapable of hiding the life that was so monstrously out of step with their words. And the crowning tragedy was, they *believed* in their mask! They really considered that they were men of God in direct proportion to the truth they intellectually grasped, and so became blind to the glaring inconsistencies of their attitudes and way of life.

With chagrin, I pondered my own philosophy of life that in the past had settled for that same kind of living. An avid student of Pentecostal Christianity and a reader of all the latest deeper-life books, I had been bankrupt when it came to the actual practice of it. And when bankruptcy had finally surfaced and I had been driven to resign my church and the ministry, then, in my emptiness, God in His mercy, showed me the way—His way, not mine. It had been a little over a year since I had rediscovered the God of truth, who not only demands we practice truth, but also gives us the Spirit of truth who accomplishes in us that very thing—if we let Him. And now my recent studies had confirmed what God had taught me by having me walk through it: knowing truth is not accepting a theory but plugging into the activity of practicing that truth. The atmosphere of the early church is more that of a laboratory where theories are tested and demonstrated, than of a lecture hall where philosophies are aired.

The letters of the early church show there was no place for Christians who were merely informed on the major doctrines of the faith. It speaks only of those who have education along with a discipline that puts it into the flow of their lives, incorporating it into their experience. The process of educating and bringing men into the practice of the knowledge gained was called "making disciples." In the original Greek, the word made me think of an apprentice—one who is not merely gaining knowledge, but putting it into practice under supervision.

For my first years in Brooklyn my congregation had been made up of Norwegians, most of whom as it happened were skilled carpenters. We had often laughed over the fact that I did not know how to drive a nail in straight. When we would do any work together I would miss the nail altogether and put a dent in the wall . . . or my thumb. The reason I couldn't do it was that I never made the right kind of mistakes. I had been taught carpentry in school and knew what ought to happen when I sawed this or planed that. However, when I banged my thumb a few times, I gave up and settled for a shabby job or, more often, was bailed out by a master craftsman from the congregation. What had made them master craftsmen? Apprenticeship. They, too, had been taught the principles of carpentry and also had begun by banging their thumbs and sawing off too much. The difference was they made these mistakes under the supervision of someone who had mastered the craft, and their mistakes thus became learning experiences— platforms for explanation as to why they made the mistake, a demonstration of how to do it correctly, and another try. In short, they made the right kind of mistakes. Every mistake that they understood, took them another step away from incompetence.

This, I discovered, was the meaning of the word disciple: a learning process that involved practice and learning from the example of one more experienced who was not only telling you what to do, but showing you as he told you. In discipling another believer, the tutor is himself a disciple since *the* Teacher—the only perfect example—is Christ. Although God took to Himself our human nature in order to die for us, that One also lived out for us, in our world, a life of perfect submission to the Father, that we might model our lives upon His.

Sadly, I thought of the number who had over the years tried to practice the Christian way of life and upon a few failures had given up to become the burden of the congregation. Every emergency was simply another bailing out by the few who could have faith and had learned to practice it. The church, as I had moved among its ranks, was woefully short on disciples and abounding in hangers-on who were satisfied with a sporadic performance, or none at all.

And then sickened, I heard my own voice preaching people *into* that kind of shabby living. I remembered how I had based my call to Christ on whether a person would like to go to heaven when he died. That was merely an appeal to the self that looked out for its own good at any cost, an appeal that avoided saying that heaven was absolute obedience to God's will, and began right now, implicit in the petition, "Thy will be done on earth as it is in heaven." The call should have been calling men to repent, and enter the kingdom of Jesus Christ, and Lord of the universe. A call that demanded submission to His very real rule, being apprenticed to the Jesus way, to live out His commands by the enabling power of His Spirit within.

My message had, of necessity, emphasized forgiveness— for we were not preaching the possibility of living this way successfully without it. Failure was built in, and so, week after week we came to confess our failures, with no hope of ever really changing. We had settled for banging nails in crooked—if at all. We had missed the point. Jesus intended that we should be practitioners of the truth, being apprenticed to the Master Craftsman. I buried my head in my hands, realizing afresh what I had been delivered from the previous year, and praising Him for the quiet revolution He had begun within me.

Gradually in the days that followed, my understanding of discipleship began to be clearer. One night, I pondered the final words of Jesus in the Sermon on the Mount.

> Therefore every one who hears these words of Mine and acts upon them, may be compared to a wise man, who built his house upon the rock. And the rain descended and the floods came, and the winds blew, and burst against that house; and yet it did not fall, for it had been founded upon the rock. And every one who hears these words of Mine, and does not act upon them, will be like a foolish man, who built his house upon the sand. And the rain descended, and the floods came, and the winds blew, and burst against that house; and it fell, and great was its fall. (Matt. 7:24-27)

As I read them over and over, I realized I had been missing the point of what He was saying. I had often used this to warn people that their lives would collapse, if they did not believe on Jesus as Lord and Savior. That was true, but to *truly* believe was to *act* on what I believed. So the man on the rock was the one who heard His words and *acted on them.* The man on the sand was not merely to be dismissed as an unbeliever; Jesus defined unbelief as one who heard His words but did not act upon them.

Jesus called men to a tough commitment. Eager men had come asking to join His band, and He had solemnly warned them to count the cost. Again I cringed, as I heard myself asking an audience to bow their heads and not to look around, so that someone could put up his hand quickly and put it down again without anyone else seeing it. My message had not been to weigh the magnitude of the commitment, but rather to sneak to Jesus, while no one was looking and while you happened to be in the mood. No wonder so many of these "converts" had disappeared overnight.

Jesus did not let people "only believe"; He shattered *that* idea in my thinking while reading John 8:31, 32.

> Jesus therefore was saying to those Jews who had believed Him, "If you abide in My word, then you are truly disciples of Mine; and you shall know the truth, and the truth shall make you free."

Those who believed on Him, He urged to continue in submitted fellowship with Him, learning truth from Him and then they would know the truth and would begin to know its freeing power.

His call was to be yoked to Him and learn a new way to live.

> Come to Me, all who are weary and heavy laden, and I will give you rest. Take My yoke upon you, and learn from Me, for I am gentle and humble in heart; and you shall find rest for your souls. For My yoke is easy, and My load is light. (Matt. 11:28-30)

I was understanding more and more that to be a disciple is to die to self and begin to live His life after Him.

> Then Jesus said to His disciples, "If anyone wishes to come after Me, let him deny himself, and take up his cross, and follow me." (Matt. 16:24)

The ancient rabbis had their disciples who sat at their feet and learned of them. Their first step was to learn to chant the Law exactly as their masters did. A disciple could be identified with his rabbi by the way he intoned the Law. Jesus calls us to die to *our* way of singing life and to tone our lives after Him.

The glory of the Good News is that *that* death was accomplished for us at the cross. His death was the all-inclusive death; we all can say that He died *for* us and *as* us. Struggling hopelessly to die to self-will *is in itself an act of self-will.* Faith is not responding to a call to *do* but responding to what God has *done* in Christ. Faith is resting in the one act of Jesus *for* us that freed us forever from bondage to our self-will. Thus resting we are joined to His death and resurrection by the Spirit who comes to live mightily within us.

This union is real and final. We have died to the old kind of person we were, and are now new people, alive in union with Christ. But now we must become in our life style who we really are. We constantly face patterns of life that belong to our rebellious self-will. It is here we must choose to actualize that death to self-will that is ours in Christ. In choosing to let the Spirit live through us the life of Jesus, we die to the old self-patterns. We in fact become who we are.

This is the grace of God. What He has done for us, and continues to do *in* us if we let Him, we could never do. He has placed in us the Holy Spirit to accomplish in us the impossible life. But that doesn't make us robots. Ours is the daily choice to obey the commands of the Lord in the power of His Spirit within. We voluntarily choose to shuck off our way of life that belongs to our dead past and adopt the way of life that comes from who we really are in Christ.

Any "Grace of God" that doesn't inspire within us a "No" to sin and the old way of self is false grace. Paul defines God's grace.

27

For the grace of God that brings salvation has appeared to all men. It teaches us to say "No" to ungodliness and worldly passions, and to live self-controlled, upright and godly lives in this present age. (Titus 2:11, 12 NIV)

And he called the disciples in Philippi:

So then, my beloved, just as you have always obeyed not as in my presence only, but now much more in my absence, work out your salvation with fear and trembling. (Phil. 2:12)

The call to work out into practice the impossible life was based on the glorious certainty. . . .

For it is God who is at work in you, both to will and to work for His good pleasure. (Phil. 2:13)

In his letters Paul used a word to describe this apprenticeship. It is "train." He wrote to Timothy:

. . . train yourself to be godly. (I Tim. 4:7 NIV)

The word "train" is reminiscent of the Greek Olympic Games. It envisions a man who wishes to train for the Olympic Games. He is flabby and overweight through long-established habits of self-indulgence. Under the direction and supervision of the gym master, he begins the arduous task of getting into top physical condition. In the beginning, there is pain in the simplest exercises and disciplines as every limb violently reacts to the change of habits. Each muscle has to die out to an old life style. At times in the early days of training there are often moments when the man is exhausted and discouraged and wants to quit. But the gym master knows his man and has tailored the program to fit him and knows exactly how far to extend him.

Then one day he notices that he can do the basic exercises without his arms and legs feeling like lead and his lungs searing with fire. In fact he is enjoying it and a new radiance of fitness begins to come over him after the training sessions. Now he looks forward with enthusiasm to each session as the gym master begins to work on the finer points of his style, continuing to extend him, right up to the day when he will take a gold medal.

This is not a theory of fitness, but an entering into a total program with a master gymnast who is the model of what he teaches and who is able to teach even the most undisciplined how to exercise and to win.

Ours is this kind of training, under the Holy Spirit with a view to godliness. He doesn't require natural ability; He has trained the lame, and even the blind. All He demands is total surrender and so warns the applicant to count the cost.

So Ray wanted to be educated in the Bible? The great danger was that he would return bloated with knowledge that he had not put into practice, dangerously untested theories of holy life. Such knowledge was poison, for it could fester into pride, causing him to despise those less knowledgeable. This miracle of grace would have turned into idolatry; the worship of his knowledge of the truth, as if such knowledge qualified him to claim he walked with God.

No. I felt that God had shown me that Ray—and thousands like him—must be discipled. Their knowledge must come with apprenticeship, plenty of supervised labwork in everyday life. Until we could find a school where we knew this would happen, we advised him to continue driving the cab.

When Ray applied for baptism, I was satisfied he knew

29

what he was doing, and also inwardly thrilled that *I* knew in a way I had not known before. As a church we had always baptized believers by total immersion, but baptism had never meant so much as it had come to mean over the past year, and the past few weeks had brought it all together.

Ray was a dead-alive boy. His death was achieved not by meditation on nothingness or fasting from sleep and food. In fact, the miracle was through nothing he had done, but by resting on the declaration of what God had accomplished for man in the one representative man, Jesus Christ. He was dead—not into nothingness, but into Life, to live with the life of Jesus Christ within him, in the presence of the Holy Spirit.

Baptism was a presentation for burial. The man who had lived this life of sin under the authority of Satan, and in obedience to the passions of the flesh with its hatreds, bitterness and resentment—that man was dead, and now it was time to acknowledge that in burial.

The world looked on Ray as a dead one. The Ray they had known had mysteriously died and had been replaced by someone else. The new person was certainly the old Ray as to body shell and personality, but so under the direction of another life as to be hardly recognizable. It was not that he was suppressing the old life either, it was more and more being *replaced* by the Spirit of Christ.

When the immediate circle of the world heard that he was to be baptized, the act had meaning to them. They could not have put it into words, but they knew that this confirmed their worst suspicions—he really *was* dead, and the funeral was to take place in Salem Tabernacle. At first, they had thought he was on another trip—into another fad, said some of his relatives. But this was the finale. The independent, do-it-yourself Ray Ciervo had died and now lived a new life in union with Christ.

For Ray, it *was* a statement of burial. He was saying a joyful farewell to the world to which he had already died. Baptism brought together in one act of faith all that he had come to believe in his heart. It was the God-ordained way of making the statement of all that he had come to see, culminating in the life-changing fact that Jesus Christ was now Lord. The vines and clinging tentacles of the world were now acknowledged as dead things in his life; the long roots of the world's ways would continue to be found in his life as the years unrolled, but they were dead and could be pulled out and discarded. The life of the Spirit was all that counted now.

On the Sunday night he was baptized, Ray stood between Floyd and myself in the water. In front of us was the congregation of Salem, joyful at the long line of fellows and girls waiting to be baptized. We laid hands on him and prayed that he might receive the Holy Spirit in fullness. It wasn't a death life, I told him and the others, but rather an abundant life. We were not called only to a list of negative "giving ups," but glorious positive "putting ons." Not just dying out to one life style, but coming alive to a new dimension of holy and supernatural living, all of which is in the Holy Spirit.

In that moment I felt we were somehow directly linked to the early church.

This Jesus God raised up again, to which we are all witnesses. Therefore having been exalted to the right hand of God, and having received from the Father the promise of the Holy Spirit, He has poured forth this which you both see and hear. . . . Repent, and let each of you be baptized in the name of Jesus Christ for the forgiveness of your sins; and you shall receive the gift of the Holy Spirit. For the promise is for you and

31

your children, and for all who are far off, as many as the Lord our God shall call to Himself. (Acts 2:32-33, 38-39)

We plunged him into the water. He came up dripping and unable to see clearly. We guided him to the steps of the pool, and a brother threw a towel over him and helped him down into the changing rooms.

The congregation began to sing from Colossians 3:1 *If ye then be risen with Christ.* I looked at the boy going down the stairs, and in the moment before the next candidate stepped into the water, I became acutely aware of another truth we had just acted out. Ray had placed himself in our hands. He could not baptize himself; he needed the help of the Body of Christ. Without us, he could not have adequately obeyed God and moved on in the walk of faith. He had come out of the water unable to see clearly, needing us to guide him and put him into the ready arms of another brother.

It seemed the Spirit said to me, *He is in your hands—you are to teach him all that I have taught you.*

After the service I went to my office, closed the door, and sat down uneasy in my spirit. *He is in your hands* rang in my head. That was more responsibility than I cared for. Surely I was to tell him to rest in the hands of the Lord, to be a disciple of Jesus, and obey Him in all things.

But then, how did anyone get apprenticed in the kingdom of God? If the Lord did it directly without using men of God on earth, He hadn't done a very good job with a lot of us! I admitted to myself fearfully that it was too vague to say that we are just disciples of Jesus. The Jesus who walked the roads of Galilee, discipling that group of men was not here—and the very word disciple demanded someone *here*. A man could not apprentice himself anymore than he could baptize himself.

Very well, I argued, but the Holy Spirit *is* here now, God on earth; in fact Jesus said that He would come to take His place as teacher. It is *His* job to disciple. But the question presented itself, where is the Spirit—is He a disembodied vapor? "The Spirit is in the Body of Christ" I answered myself aloud. Then it dawned on me. The Body must disciple, for that is where Christ by the Spirit is today. To simply say that the Lord would teach Ray and the others was nothing more than a refusal to face up to responsibility. That Lord was in us, in me, and was making it plain that He was about to disciple Ray *through* us.

I considered what I now understood of discipleship. It meant Ray was to be taught truth, but in such a way that he could watch it worked into my life, and then explained if he needed help in allowing it to work in his circumstances. But I still felt uncomfortable with such a situation. We had always turned attention away from ourselves, and any mention of the help or encouragement a person had gained from our example had been squashed with, "It is not me, but the Lord"—which made everyone embarrassed to bring it up again. Because only God could be trusted, we counseled new converts to never get their eyes on man.

Was it *God* telling me that Ray was to apprentice himself to *me*? The very thought was the height of arrogance and pride on my part. There was something here, no doubt, and time would tell, but for now I knew my call—I would teach from behind a pulpit and leave the working-out to the Holy Spirit. The responsibility of apprenticing I preferred to leave where it belonged, with Jesus.

IV

"Why not?" The voice on the other end of the phone was obviously puzzled. "It would be a great experience for them to get out and witness." It was a youth pastor from the outskirts of the city. He had called to ask if the group of newly-saved hippies that he had heard were coming to Salem, could conduct a youth rally for him on the edge of the metropolitan area.

"I'm sorry, but I'd rather they not participate. Not just yet."

His perplexity turned to annoyance. "Look! There will be at least a thousand kids there, maybe more if they hear these ex-hippies are coming. They need to hear where your kids have come from, and it will be a marvelous experience for your kids to witness."

I shook my head as I listened. Two years ago that could have been me at his end of the phone, eager to get a group of ex-hippies to come and tell of their life in sin, personally enjoying the crowd their presence would draw. I realized now, that such a crowd could easily slip into enjoying sin by proxy in such testimonies. "I'm not sure your thousand kids need to hear where these fellows and girls have come from, any more than they need to rehash it. Isn't it a little like keeping garbage around the house, and turning the trash can out for the neighbors to see yesterday's eating habits?"

In the silence that followed, I wondered if I was acting self-righteously. I didn't mean to. "My biggest concern is for our kids, though," I continued. "They may have a sensational story, but they are not ready to give witness before thousands, and they have nothing new to share with those thousands. You see. . . ."

"Not *ready*?" he almost shouted. "They're saved, aren't they? Isn't that qualification enough? Listen, if you want to keep youth in the church, you've got to give them something to do. You're stifling them. You've got to use them or lose them. I'd take any one of them as my youth leader right now."

I had heard the cliches before, and wondered idly if we had been at the same conference that guaranteed the same results.

"Say, they're not members of your church, are they?"

"No," I said wanly.

"Why don't you let me call them? I'll see what *they* say!"

What was the use? I couldn't tell this brother what I had learned and seen. He wasn't asking the questions, so how could he hear the answers? Anyway, I could hardly put into words what I was trying to say. "I say that they are not ready yet, they need. . . ." I stopped, groping for words. "They need to be apprenticed," I blurted out, regretting it instantly.

"They need *what*?" he squawked.

"I promise you this much," I said. "I'll let them make up their own minds. It will be their decision. If they want, they can call you." And the soft purr of the dial tone was his only reply.

Slowly I replaced the receiver in its cradle. What I had said was the logical conclusion of all I had been discovering in the word *disciple*. It was obvious that I did not know where I was *going;* all I did know was where I had come *from.*

Six of them sitting on the few chairs in my office and cross-legged on the floor. There was Michael who had been led to Christ by Ray, and who, in turn, had brought Pattie and Chris. Steve, Lee and Ray completed the group. I told them of the phone call and reaction, explaining as best I could.

"You see," I said, almost apologetically, "you're not really ready for that. However strong you feel, you don't know the first things of Christianity. To minister to others, the Scriptures say, you have got to have had some experience or you will fall because of pride. That's how the devil fell."

They nodded, understanding. They would explain it to the others. Chris grinned, her smile filling her face. Her smile was always disarming, and her eyes, behind her enormous round glasses, sparkled with life. "Whatever you say, shepherd. We're your sheep!"

Ray added quietly, "One day, I know I will minister, but I also know that I need teaching first and I'm more than willing to receive."

As I later talked about that conversation with my wife, Jean, I marveled. "Before their conversion, these kids were unbelievably rebellious. They took orders from nobody. Now they meekly submit to us and trust us to teach them what they need to know."

"That puts quite a responsibility on your shoulders," she said bluntly.

The fears I felt surfaced, but I brushed them aside. "You didn't have to say that," I said laughing weakly.

The sun was getting warmer, that May of 1972. New York City would be a steaming jungle of concrete and steel by July. But this morning the air was pleasantly warm, the sky an azure blue and the trees on Ridge Boulevard a bright green. It was a morning that dragged a fellow from bed, demanding to be lived. The night before we had had overflow crowds in southern Jersey. They had listened for over an hour to teaching from the Scripture. I was feeling like a true son of God in a heavenly dimension.

I walked jauntily to the side door and shouted "Praise God!" to the janitor, John Andersen, who was painting the church railings. I smiled at his carefully lettered sign on the gate. "Vet Paint," it said.

"Pastor Smit," he called after me, "Dere's someone to see you downstairs. Von of da new boys."

Opening the door of the basement, I saw Ray reading a book. He looked up and smiled. As our eyes met I realized the bond that God had forged between us.

Without preamble he announced matter-of-factly, "You've got yourself a disciple."

I stood still suddenly feeling the day drain out of me. I felt threatened. Behind a pulpit with hundreds of people wanting to be taught I was confident in God and unthreatened. Now this one young man stood opposite me and announced himself as my disciple. I was afraid. "Oh?" I managed.

"You said that I cannot and should not minister until I am trained, and I agree. You also said that there is no place that the elders feel I could go to, right now, and I believe you. So, here I am. *You* train me. I am in your hands."

I caught my breath. *I am in your hands* . . . it echoed the words of the Spirit, the night he was baptized. *He is in your hands.*

We went into the office and talked about discipleship and how we might work it out between him, Floyd, and myself. He told me he knew beyond a shadow of a doubt that God had called him to some kind of full-time ministry.

A couple of months before he had been in a prayer meeting when the words *I am the Way* were implanted in his spirit. Along with that came the impression that he was called to full-time ministry. He turned this over and over in his mind for a number of weeks. Then in early May came a convention that attracted ministers and delegates from all over the nation. One of them was E. C. Erikson, a father among us and a pioneer of many churches in the Midwest over the past fifty years. We affectionately referred to him as "E.C." Now he was crippled with arthritis and quite deaf, but still mighty in the Spirit.

At one service of the convention there was an utterance in an unknown tongue. Hardly had the speaker finished when E.C. was on his feet speaking the interpretation. Every interpretation of the utterance of tongues is a miracle, but this was doubly so, for E.C. had not heard the tongue and was speaking at the prompting of the Spirit.

His words were addressed to the crowd that filled the auditorium, but it came in a specific way to Ray bowed in his seat. "You've heard your calling from the voice within saying, 'I am the Way.' " Peace filled Ray. He knew that He who was His life and His way within was undoubtedly directing him to full-time service. Apart from his own testimony, his life over the past months had indicated a total dedication to Jesus Christ the Lord. We decided to give him biblical studies and either Floyd or myself would be with him as often as possible.

"What about your expenses? If you are sponging off your parents and calling it a faith-walk, we couldn't go on."

He nodded, "From the day I was saved, I have saved every dime and have enough money to support myself for the rest of the year."

I looked at Ray a moment without speaking. He had the dedication of a disciple, no pretensions about himself and was willing to learn. And he had already submitted in his spirit to do whatever we asked of him. There was no question that he was ready. I wished that I felt the same way about myself.

And so it began. Each morning Ray studied Romans. He examined each verse and after prayer and endless questions, he wrote out what he understood. He soon began to grasp the grace of God that he saw there. Each afternoon he spent time in prayer or accompanied Floyd or me as we did our church work. Other times, with a satchel full of booklets, he headed for the streets and parks to share Christ with his old friends.

Throughout the summer we drank coffee and ate lunch together, walked and drove and laughed together. He shared his questions, and we answered as best we knew how. He shared his problems, and we let him in on ours and worked them out together.

The first issue of discipleship is submission. The word means "to stand under," and unlike the word surrender which implies being conquered, this means a *voluntary* act of standing under another. Jesus placed it in the first basic marks of a disciple in Matthew 5. He summed it up in the word meek, which basically is an attitude of submission to God that expresses itself toward men. The miracle that the Spirit had worked in all of these young hippies was a change right there, in their willingness to stand under. Where they once bitterly hated all authority, now they were submissive and content. To be free from something is not enough however; we must know why, or we may find it cropping up again. They had to understand it and work it yet in a few areas of life.

Rebellion is everyone's problem. Isaiah 53:6 sees it as the heart of sin. "We have turned everyone to his own way" (KJV). We all tend to see ourselves as the right ones against whom all others must be judged. In our hearts, as sinners, we submit to no one. But in the rebirth, we repent, change our minds, begin to see things in the light of truth, and submit to the Lordship of Jesus Christ. This expresses itself toward authority in the world, and also to the fellowship of Christians with whom we meet, in particular, to those whom God has set over us to teach us. The first mark of a disciple is willingness to submit to another and learn.

One mid-summer day Ray came into the office looking perplexed. "Someone told me I ought to get my hair cut. What should I do?"

I laughed, "Why did they tell you that?"

"They said that it was a mark of the world, and I should be separated in my dress."

"Do you think that's true? What is your heart saying to you now?"

He looked at me, pondering the question. Then quietly, "My heart says I am separated, because I am submitted in my heart to Jesus Christ as Lord. My hair has nothing to do with it."

"Amen," I responded. "We are saved by what God has done in Christ, not by haircuts." I sipped my coffee and looked at him again. "Could it *ever* have anything to do with it?"

40

He thought for a long time. "No. Hair is only hair. The same as my jeans and sandals."

I shook my head, "Not always. When did you begin dressing like this and wearing your hair long?"

"I guess when I came back from Nam."

"Why did you do it then? Was it just the fashionable thing to do?"

"No, it was because I hated the system, and I wanted everyone to know I was different."

"Then you do see how your heart and your hair could come together?"

He looked perplexed.

"You wore long hair and a certain dress as a badge, a uniform, if you like, that told the world you hated authority and were in active rebellion."

He smiled, "Okay, so when I leave the army, I dump the uniform. But what if I am no longer bitter against authority, and have just gotten to like it this way?"

"Fine, Ray, nothing wrong with long hair and jeans, if it isn't a uniform to identify you. Keep open to what the Spirit may say to you about it and we'll talk it over later."

The question of authority and submission had to be worked out at a very practical level. Theory alone would go like water off a duck's back. For most of the group it came to a head one evening when they were all gathered after a home Bible study. We sat around talking and drinking Cokes, when someone asked if we could pray that the police would not find out about his van that had been used for smuggling cigarettes.

When I pointed out that God had ordained the police and anointed them, there was a howl of protest. I knew it was time to answer a question that was finally being asked in the Holy Spirit's good timing. They were in submission but

41

didn't know why, and had no peace, for they themselves were presently conducting their lives.

I had them read Romans 13:1-7 from J.B. Phillips' translation.

Every Christian ought to obey the civil authorities for all legitimate authority is derived from God's authority, and the existing authority is appointed under God. To oppose authority then is to oppose God, and such opposition is bound to be punished.

The honest citizen has no need to fear the keepers of law and order, but the dishonest man will always be nervous of them. If you want to avoid this anxiety just lead a law-abiding life, and all that can come your way is a word of approval. The officer is God's servant for your protection. But if you are leading a wicked life you have reason to be alarmed. The "power of the law" which is vested in every legitimate officer, is no empty phrase. He is, in fact, divinely appointed to inflict God's punishment upon evil-doers.

You should, therefore, obey the authorities, not simply because it is the safest, but because it is the right thing to do. It is right, too, for you to pay taxes for the civil authorities are appointed by God for the good purposes of public order and well-being. Give everyone his legitimate due, whether it be rates, or taxes, or reverence, or respect!

For a moment or two no one said anything. And then the questions came. "What about when the police are corrupt and liars?" "What about persecution?" "What if the government forbids the reading of the Bible?"

I waited till a lull came, then explained the fact that *we* submit to the office, and *God* deals with the man who may be corruptly filling that office. Paul and Peter never tried to overthrow the emperor Nero, in spite of his corruption and degeneracy. They prayed for Nero and believed God was in it all.

"What about when the government forbids worship?" insisted a voice from the corner.

"We submit up to the point where they forbid us to worship or command us to break God's commandment. Then we tell them that we must obey God rather than man. However, we immediately submit to their punishment and praise God!"

The conversation drifted on, some actually coming to a decision to go to the police and confess to certain crimes or misdemeanors. All admitted they could see very clearly that the Lordship of Jesus had been worked out in their lives that night in a far-reaching way.

The next day, over lunch, Ray looked up from his hamburger. "I've been thinking and praying about my hair. Last night's conversation put a lot together for me, and I realize even better now what I have come out of. I know I'm not in rebellion, and I guess one day I will cut my hair. I might even wear a suit! But for now I am going to keep it long."

I asked him why keep it long now, if he planned to cut it one day.

"When we first came to Salem, we were the only ones with long hair. We felt so odd and out of place that it was only God's grace that kept us going. I really believe that if I keep it long, it will help any others who wander in feel more at home." The months ahead proved he was absolutely right.

After lunch, as I drove to the church, I thought of the areas being taught at a depth that was maturing these young people to where they could share their faith, as they lived steadily to God, without the danger of it becoming an ego

43

trip. I silently thanked God for His perfect provision. Soon they would be prepared to minister to others, but only after they truly knew why and how they were Christians. "You've got to have more than just a salvation experience; you've got to *know* why, so you can impart it to others."

"Pardon?" said Ray.

"Oh, nothing. Just praising God for saving you from an empty life."

Not long after that, it came to me quite vividly that answering a question while relaxing in someone's apartment, or talking of life in relation to truth over lunch in a diner, was actually much closer to the ways of Jesus than those in a formal church setting. The thought stayed with me for days. I knew it was something I had to follow up.

V

July came with its camp meetings. I was to speak at the Elim Camp in Lima, near Rochester, New York, where a strong bond of love had been forged between us over the months. The camp meetings were characterized by uninhibited worship and hours of Bible teaching, which made it one of the greatest camps on the East Coast. This year I took Ray and a number of the new converts from Brooklyn with me.

As I stood up to teach the congregation one night, I had a strong urge to teach a chorus that had unusually blessed the Brooklyn church. Never very sure of myself in teaching new songs, I called those who had traveled with me to come to the platform.

It is doubtful if the platform had ever been graced by a group like the one which now approached it. Over the years, Elim had taken a strong stand on clothes and hair. Girls were forbidden to wear blue jeans, and boys were forbidden to wear their hair long. It seemed to me that every long-haired boy and blue-jeaned girl in the building was coming up onto the platform, and they were all from my congregation. I shut my eyes, unable to bear the look of shock on the faces of some of the saints. I strained my ears to catch a hoped-for Amen from Carlton Spencer, the principal.

We began to sing the chorus, and my fears melted away in the worship. I realized I was proud of God's grace in these boys and girls, and that I was committed to them, one with them, and proud to be a trophy of God's grace along with them. The congregation rose to join us, and we were all caught up in a spirit of praise. Our love for each other was deeper from that day on.

The students on the Elim campus quickly made friends with our people and when we arrived back in Brooklyn, everyone wanted to have Bible training. The growth in Ray had been obvious to all since he had been studying with us, and now the other young people wanted to be trained too. The conversation with Elim students had fanned the smoldering fire of our interest in Bible study. Mike and Ray came as a deputation, and asked that we open a school in the basement of the church to train everyone the same way we were training Ray. Floyd and I listened and promised we would let them know.

Floyd was ready and eager to start as soon as possible. He had been a lecturer and administrator in a Bible school in Chicago, and we had often talked of Bible education since he had arrived in the city. Within a few days he had worked out the cost of running such a school and the cost per student.

I did not fully share his enthusiasm. We had tried before to have a Bible school in the church. It had taken the form of an evening school that was to run for a period of nine weeks. It was to cover a variety of subjects and enthusiasm ran high from our own membership and from surrounding churches. But that was back in the days before I had handed over the running of the church to the Holy Spirit. From the beginning, it had been our work, part of our vain efforts to produce a New Testament church. By the second week, the enthusiasm had drained. We were lecturing out of a sense of duty, the students were bored, and wondered why they had signed up at all. For all concerned, the evenings had become sheer drudgery, and by the sixth week the school had sunk without a trace. "Malcolm's folly," they called it. I still felt shame in having to admit that it had been a complete fiasco. And so I was more than a little uneasy about starting another school. Floyd wanted this one to hold classes during the day and last for two years.

Floyd and I talked about it by the hour. We gradually realized that we were at a major crossroad in the life of the church, and in our own lives. Later as I sat in my office I was forcibly reminded that things had changed since the last abortive attempt at Christian education. The Holy Spirit was now in control, and as long as we were aiming towards His goals and following the flow of His life, we could not fail. It was foolish to compare the results of our efforts in the past with what the Holy Spirit was seeking to do today.

We decided to go to the Adirondack Mountains to fast and pray as we had often done recently when faced with major decisions. We also took Dennis Hunt along with us. He was the New York City leader of a group of students from Elim Bible Institute who came periodically to the city for on-the-street training. He wanted to get away and enjoy the presence of God, and it would make good fellowship for us.

We spent much time alone and came together only for communion and sharing. Alone in my bedroom, I faced up to where we were going. The previous year I had spoken at a charismatic conference in Pittsford, near Rochester, New York, and that had become an open door to multitudes of

47

people, hungry for the Word of God in other parts of the East Coast. As I knelt by the bed, I remembered the hungry crowds which had come to the teachings week after week in New Jersey. At the invitation of a few businessmen, I had gone to the basement of an Episcopal Church in Ramsey to give Bible teaching, and the numbers quickly outgrew it and many other church auditoriums after it. An average of six hundred came week after week, devouring every word the Lord gave me. I remembered the Holiday Inn in Hazlet, New Jersey, that was packed each week. Was I to give all that up for a handful of boys and girls, fresh from the streets? Could I handle both a school and the increasing bookings? I doubted it.

And the cold truth was, I felt threatened in the presence of one or two people. It was strange; in front of a large audience I could relax and flow in the Spirit, but facing one person sometimes left me speechless. The Lord kept before my mind the fact that Jesus addressed the multitudes but gave Himself to training a small group of twelve. I was very willing to obey His command to teach, but frankly fearful with His methods of doing it so totally in a small group.

I thought of something else as I walked in the warm sunlit woods: was I creating a cold institution where the Bible was taught as a science, a beautiful theory? Increasingly I was seeing that there was more to the Bible than just true words. The Pharisees had had the Old Testament, had memorized all the true words, *and had totally missed the truth* when He came. They had the words and missed the Word Himself.

To know the Scripture, and not to fellowship with the Christ who fills it, is to be guilty of idolatry, of worshiping the book called the Bible. To study the Bible and its doctrines and not to practice them in everyday living is the worst form of religious hypocrisy. I remembered, in Eng-

48

land, brothers who wouldn't speak to brothers because they disagreed on fine points of doctrine regarding the second coming of Christ. They were so obsessed with being right they cut their brothers in Christ dead to prove it. I shrank from the possibility of producing a group of religious nit-pickers.

But up in the mountains, kneeling, with Floyd and Dennis on the threadbare carpet, and singing praise to God around a cup of wine and a tray of broken bread, I admitted to myself that I knew where the River of Life within me was flowing. What the Spirit had begun to do in Ray, could, given the time, be done in a multitude. It *was* possible to teach truth and teach it in the context of life and practice.

But even as I knew it I wondered about the crowds. Could I let those thousands of people go for a handful in a basement? Later, when alone, I tried to put it in words to the Lord. Walking deep into the woods I poured out what was so deep in my heart. "Lord, I can't give up my ministry of teaching the charismatic renewal for so few. It's the ministry you have given me." I stopped speaking, and in the intense silence of the forest, I heard a replay in my mind of what I had just said. Two words seemed to echo as in a great cavern—*my ministry.*

What a fool! It was not *my* ministry! Hadn't I died out to such monumental egoism? It was *His* ministry, and He could do with it as He pleased. He could use me to minister to thousands, or tens or even one or none at all for that matter. How foolish to try to protect my ministry. God, who gave it, was its strength and its goal! I laughed aloud, feeling lighter than I had in days and joyfully embraced this opportunity to take up the cross and move on into the Resurrection Life.

That night, sitting around the log fire, the music of a

million crickets and frogs came through the screen door as we began to talk of the school in concrete terms and work out what we would teach.

Driving out of the woods and down into the city, I knew my life was going to be very different. I would be anchored now, controlled by a commitment to a group of young fellows and girls in blue jeans. Our aim was to give content to the experience the students already had. Beginning with teaching on how to interpret the Scripture, we set out a course that covered every major doctrine and every book in the Bible. We interspersed the daily lectures with an hour of waiting on God and of learning to fellowship together. We divided the lecture load between us, and invited Osborne Arnes from Staten Island to help with a few hours.

We shared with the church our understanding that it was the responsibility of the church to train its elders and missionaries within the congregation rather than send them away to an artificial situation. The congregation responded enthusiastically, and we decided to begin in six weeks, early in September. Now that we were actually committed, we were disappointed that the applications for the school were so few. Too many wanted to wait to see how it would work out. The first applicants were Ray, Mike, Lee, Chris, Susan and Mary Anne. More promised to join us later.

The first day finally came. It was seven thirty in the morning when I walked up 54th Street in the fresh crisp air of September. Ahead of me, Mike was just going into the church, a knapsack slung over his shoulder. I had no idea how to handle the first day of a Bible school, and very little idea of how it would all work out. Even so, I was confident and almost hilariously at rest in the Holy Spirit. He had started this school, He alone recognized it, and He would take it where He would.

In the basement Susie had made coffee, and Chris was pouring me a cup. Her big eyes were dancing, and her smile was wide. Whatever the next months held, there would be plenty of life around with Chris in the group. At eight o'clock a.m., we moved into the Sunday school room, set up in the corner of the basement. Suddenly, I felt afraid. It was a dismal room with frosted windows. Even if we opened them, all that we could see was a dingy alley. A large antiquated air conditioner sagged in the far window precariously supported by the top of a cupboard piled with Sunday school material. The partition separating us from the rest of the basement was dark brown, the walls an institutional cream. Even though we were so few, the long, narrow room seemed to be crowding in on us. For a moment I had a picture of vast crowds of charismatics jammed into large air-conditoned buildings across the nation. Here I was, trapped in a dismal basement in Brooklyn, having committed the next years of my life to these two boys and four girls. The moment passed as quickly as it came. I really loved these who were now my students. So thoroughly had I enjoyed being with them, I often forgot I was their pastor.

We began by beginning. Committing the whole school to God in prayer, I began to give an introduction to theology, as we were going to teach it.

It is impossible to know God, until you know God. We were not setting out to clinically examine a God who lived in textbooks. In a sense we had already begun *knowing* Him by faith in Jesus Christ. We lived with Him, as He lived in us. What we were coming to know now was *Who* we knew.

I was warming to my theme, when the door at the far end of the partition opened. It never opened easily, and this time it threatened to bring the partition down with it. It was Sandy, rather red in the face, who finally came through the opening. That summer she had worked with Mary Anne on the streets in Greenwich Village, rescuing addicts and running a coffee house. I had forgotten she was coming, as she had been away in Syracuse for most of the last month. Now she apologized for being late. She smiled and blushed as she talked, "I have a friend with me—" and reaching out through the door, pulled in another girl. She, too, was dressed in jeans, her black hair windswept around her pale face. She looked at me through thick glasses and said, "Please, may I come to your school? My name is Joanne."

VI

What follows is Joanne's story, not as she briefly shared it that day, but as we came to know it in the process of coming to know her.

A chill wind tugged at her black hair, and she pulled her faded denim jacket tightly around her slim frame. Shivering, she willed Tinky to come out from behind the great doors of the church.

What did people do in there anyway? It was a part of Tinky's life that Joanne had never understood or cared to inquire into. What anyone would want to do in a gloomy building with a handful of old ladies was beyond her. All she knew was that on any Sunday morning, Tinky could be found in the large Baptist church, sandwiched between the high rises on East 57th Street in Manhattan.

Jo had not planned to be in New York this particular Sunday. In fact, she had not planned to be anywhere in particular. Finding herself in the city, she had decided to give Tinky a surprise. A smile flickered around her lips.

Surprise! She wondered what the reaction of the old ladies would be when those doors opened, and they saw her. As she stood on the pavement, she melted into the multi-cultured East Side scene. The few people who were stirring on Sunday morning at 11:45 didn't notice the wind-swept hippie. She was just part of the New York furniture.

Now she looked down at her clothes, aware that her faded jeans and crumpled clothing, creased more than usual because of sleeping in the car for two nights, would be very noticeable to the church people. Would Tinky be embarrassed? Her long hair under the red headband had not seen a comb for two days. "And," she muttered to herself, "I could probably use a shower." She peered through her thick glasses at the doors and wished for the end of whatever they started in there at eleven.

She had waited so long that when the doors actually did open, they caught her off guard. Seconds later, a large cheerful crowd spilled out into the watery sunlight of the late fall day. What in—where were the few old ladies? She had little time to be shocked, for she stood directly in the path of the flood. Suddenly, she was a parrot in a flock of sparrows. Ladies in fur coats and neat outfits, with hair immaculately in place swept past her accompanied by men in conservative suits and raincoats, and short, carefully combed hair. Many of the men carried funny little black cases under their arms and everyone looked terribly important and fussy. How could so many "straights" get together?

Where is Tinky? What was she doing in a crowd like this? Joanne searched the faces that moved past her. Some stared icily at the strange girl among them, others gave her wide berth. *Am I a leper?* A few smiled and said, "God bless you." Joanne nodded back, embarrassed. *Tinky, where are you?*

The crowd gradually thinned, and finally no one came

through the doors. The dark hole beyond seemed to be empty. Hesitantly she stepped inside and looked in. There was no one there but an usher, who quickly moved toward her, reminding her absurdly of police at a rock festival. Confused, she retreated.

Back on the sidewalk she hesitated. "Looking for someone?" a friendly male voice inquired. Turning, she saw an older man standing in a doorway. From the tidy appearance and the short slicked-back hair she concluded he must be one of those people from inside the church. It was his tie that made her giggle—a knot so small, and two thin ends that disappeared under his top overcoat button. At his feet was a black case. Whatever did these people carry into church? Her first reaction was to back off. Was this creep trying to pick her up?

"I'm waiting for someone, too," he volunteered, and she found herself almost liking the honesty of his open face.

"I'm looking for a girl called . . ." she hesitated, groping for her real name and not being able to recall it, "called Tinky. She was supposed to be in there," she nodded toward the church. "I don't suppose you'd happen to know her, would you?" she asked, not really expecting he would.

"Sorry" the man smiled, "I was in the service this morning, but I'm afraid I've never heard of anyone by that name."

She shivered and turned to go. The man picked up his case and fell in beside her. "Look, my friend hasn't turned up, either. You look hungry; would you join me for lunch? By the way," he added smiling, "my name is Richard Frank."

Jo was startled by his disarming friendliness, and found herself trusting him. At the mention of food, she became aware of the gnawing in her stomach. Coffee and rolls had been her diet for two days—and not so much of that because she had to keep enough money for the two tanks of gas it would take to get her home.

"O.K.," she heard herself saying, "my name is Joanne Ferreira. I'm from Boston."

Richard guided her through the sparse Sunday crowd, to the Yangtze River Restaurant. *I can't go in there dressed like this,* she thought. But Richard waited patiently holding the door for her; he didn't seem to realize that she was a hippie and didn't belong in this plush place. The maitre d' stared at her stonily and led them to a table in a corner.

The restaurant was warm and the food was unbelievably good. She gulped it down like a starving waif paying little attention to Richard's steady flow of conversation. Occasionally she interjected an "uh huh" or a nod where it seemed appropriate, but without the faintest idea of what he was talking about. It was something about God loving her, and Jesus Christ dying for her. But she was only interested in the food in front of her, and not in what he had to say.

They finished the meal, he paid the bill, and they both left the restaurant. She thanked him, said goodbye to him at the street corner, and went to find her car. She had to be back in Boston by the next morning.

Strange guy, she thought, as she headed the car north out of the city. Strange day! What was she doing in New York today anyway? For that matter, what was she doing, period? Was there any meaning to this series of events called life? It was a strange depression, an unexplainable misery that had driven her on this weekend, as on all the others.

After she had closed the university bookstore Friday, she had headed out, not knowing—or caring—where. Albany, Buffalo, or even Syracuse, where she had grown up; it didn't matter. This weekend it happened to be New York.

She had been in and out of college, and had finally dropped out because of her excursions into the drug world. LSD had taken her on too many trips to stay in school. It was the emptiness and misery that had clung to her like a layer of smog and had driven her to begin checking out the drug scene. Following her parents to Boston, she took a job as a clerk in the bookstore on the campus of Boston University. By a strange series of coincidental breaks, she had become the manager of the store at the age of nineteen. She controlled the acquisition of all Boston University textbooks and had a staff of thirty-five working under her. The previous year, more than a million dollars worth of books had passed through her hands.

She had to admit that things could not be going better than they were. Her parents never interfered, and now, at twenty, she couldn't go much further in what she was doing. Then why did she feel so miserable? There was no answer—anymore now than at any time in the past two years. Unless no answer was itself an answer. There *was* no meaning to life. Pressing her lips together she stepped down on the accelerator and the car shot ahead. She wanted to grab some sleep before opening the store tomorrow.

Suddenly, the road disappeared in an engulfing blackness. *What! Is this a flashback? It's going to kill me.* The thought paralyzed her as the car sped on in total darkness. Her mouth opened to scream, but even before the sound came she was braking and easing the car to the right.

She felt the right wheels begin to ride on the rough and held the wheel steady until she had almost stopped, then put the left wheels over too. "My *God,* what's happening to me?" The darkness thinned to a gray mist, and then she could see again. Her trembling hand switched off the engine and she sat sweating, feeling like she was about to throw up. All was still, except for the rush of a passing truck that rocked the car.

She found herself frantically reliving the nightmare of what had just happened. What had she said at the end? She had used the word "God" often enough as a curse or out of fright and frustration. But the way she had said it this time returned to her mind again and again even more than the fear of blindness. *My God, what's happening to me?* She had never addressed God before, as a person who was actually listening. This time, she knew she had.

With that incredible thought, she was gripped by the sense of Someone's presence, Someone to whom she had addressed a question that she realized pertained to far more than a few seconds of sudden, harrowing blindness. And sitting there in the early twilight of that fall afternoon, the bare trees black against the pale gold of the setting sun behind her, she committed herself to the God who had arrested her and let her know He was there.

Sometime later she started the car and moved carefully back into the outside lane. Inside, she was quietly excited.

It was Tuesday. Sitting in her office, Joanne looked over the endless rows of books. There had to be *something* in all that literature that could tell her about God. Someone must have been zapped as she had, or maybe there was a biography of God somewhere. She had to know what had happened, and who this God was. She had thought about talking to a professor in the theology department, but then had dismissed the idea. Nothing very lively was going on in *that* department!

As soon as the store closed, she began going through the books, poring over anything that remotely spoke of God, or of an experience like hers. By the end of the week, she realized there was nothing in the store that could be of help to her. Yet in all of her disappointment and confusion the sense of the strange flow of life inside never left her. Her depression had really gone, and with it all desire for drugs.

"Isn't there any book that tells about God? There *must* be, somewhere. . . ." Then, in her mind, she saw the crowd in Manhattan, carrying the mysterious black bags. *Bibles!* Of course! She had never read one, but she knew it talked a lot about God. By the next day she had bought one and was eagerly reading it. The desire to know who had arrested her on the Thruway carried her through the pages she didn't understand, until she reached the Gospels. They were like streams of fresh water. Now she understood that God had come for her as Jesus Christ—in fact, He had died for her and was now alive, and His Spirit was with her. That must have been the presence she felt in the car. Now she found that she began to remember snatches of Richard Frank's conversation in the New York restaurant. So this is what he was talking about! With every new page, she committed herself to the Christ who was becoming more and more real.

She began to talk about the God she knew, and the Christ she had met through reading the Gospels to everyone she met. No one understood. One even said knowingly, "Poor Jo—too much LSD."

Where could she turn? She dismissed with a shrug the churches scattered through the city. She knew they were not for her. Her only thought was to return to New York and find Tinky. Maybe she would understand, or at least listen sympathetically. The next weekend she turned her car south on the Thruway and drove into Manhattan in time to meet Tinky as she came out of the church on East 57th Street.

Later in Tinky's apartment, Jo poured out all that had happened to her since she was last in the city. Tinky nodded, her eyes glowing with enthusiasm. "God is real, Jo! You have met Him, and you're going to find thousands who have met Him!" She went on to share how her life had come to a new birth through Jesus some years before. Climbing into bed that night Jo didn't feel so alone in her experience.

One afternoon the next week a girl came into the store looking for her. She was smiling nervously as she asked for Joanne. "Hi, my name is Sandy. I'm Tinky's cousin." Jo vaguely remembered seeing her when she had once stayed with Tinky. "Tinky was telling me that you have been saved. It's wonderful, I'm so glad."

"Saved?" Jo cut her off. "No, I guess Tinky heard wrong. Hey, what is saved?" The girl blushed and turned away in confusion. "I'm sorry, I really am—I just thought from what Tinky said . . . but I guess I have it wrong." She retreated nervously from the store, and Jo returned to her work shaking her head.

The Bible had come alive to Joanne, as though God Himself was speaking to her personally through its pages. And she had a great urge to speak to Him, to sing to Him. One night she pulled out her guitar and began strumming chords. The Bible in front of her lay open to the Book of Psalms. Flipping through the pages she found a psalm that put into words exactly what her heart now wanted to say to God. She began to strum the guitar and chords poured through her fingers. The psalm sprang into music. For weeks following that, she would sit in her room at night singing the Bible back to her God, convinced that no one else knew Him quite as well as she did.

As fall became winter, the first glow of her meeting with God gradually began to fade. "There has to be something more," she wrote in her journal.

Driving to her parents' home a few days later, she happened to notice a building set off the side of the road with the sign, "Assembly of God" neatly painted on a board outside. She hadn't noticed it before. Now a vague urge seemed to draw her to the building, and she promised herself that she would actually go there on Sunday.

The following Sunday found her sitting at the back of the little church, curiously watching what was going on. She stood out by the garb she wore, but it didn't seem to matter. From the joy-filled, free-flowing worship and spontaneous prayer, she knew that these people knew God as she did. When they announced a prayer meeting in a smaller side room, she wanted to be a part of it.

In the small room a number of people were weeping and moaning softly, saying the name of Jesus in a sobbing kind of voice. Now she began to feel uptight as some men laid their hands on the head of first one person then another. All at once they were standing in front of her. Their eyes were closed, and their hands reached out to her head. She cringed in her seat. The men began calling on Jesus, and one prayed that she would receive what he referred to as the Baptism in the Holy Spirit. As he did so, all fear left her, and a quiet joy rose within her. She felt an irrepressible desire to laugh. From deep within came a laugh of total joy, and the last traces of sadness and depression fled from her.

She became aware that there was silence in the room, and people were staring at her. Her laughter was out of place in a room so full of moans and sobs. Excusing herself, she fled to her car and drove back to her apartment in a state of holy hilarity.

A week later her car weaved through the morning traffic on Route 9 towards Boston. Inside she was joyfully singing out of her spirit the song she had composed the night before in her bedroom. As she pulled up at a traffic light, it dawned on her that she was not singing in English but in a language she had never heard before. She did not understand the words but knew they were saying all that her heart was seeking to express to God.

The days raced by after that, life now unbelievably meaningful. Again she was experiencing discontent. But it was a different kind—joyous discontent that was exciting. The thought that kept gnawing at her was that here she was, a channel for the intellectual life of thousands, all the while knowing that *that* life was not enough. *Why not sell books that talk about the Reality I know?* The thought excited her. When she had searched for books to lead her to God, she had found none. How many others were doing the same? *Why not open a bookstore full of books that would lead people to God, and have a place to rap with them and share what I know?*

The vision took hold, and a few weeks later she was driving back to Syracuse with her life savings, to open her bookstore. For four months, she tried to force the vision into reality but only succeeded in using up her savings. Discouraged, and yet still driven by what she knew to be God's voice within, she got a job in another Christian bookstore she had discovered, to help with the Christmas rush.

In the New Year, the owner, John Skinner, shared a vision that God had given him, of a bookstore on the Syracuse University campus, where the students could drop by, drink coffee and inquire about Jesus. Her spirit leaped— what he was describing was the other end of her own vision! Within a few weeks she was a part of it for real.

Within four months, through the store's ministry, forty students had come to know Christ and had been filled with the Spirit. She had at that point told them all she knew, and wondered where to take them next. She herself regularly attended the Assembly of God, but it did not occur to her to invite the converts to come with her.

Tinky had moved to Syracuse, and had been baptized with the Holy Spirit. She suggested that they go to New York City and see how her cousin Sandy was handling the problem. "She works with an organization called Teen Challenge," she explained, "and from what I've heard they have quite a follow-up with new converts." Jo smiled, remembering Sandy's embarrassment when she had denied being saved, before she even knew that that is what had happened to her. It would be good to meet her as a sister in Christ.

The June weekend in New York was invigorating. They counseled long into the night on Saturday in a coffee house in Greenwich Village that Sandy ran along with Marianne. As they dragged their weary bodies into the apartment, Sandy warned them they had to be ready by ten in the morning in order to go to church.

"Church?" croaked Jo. "You must be crazy! After going to bed at this hour?"

"That's the other end of our work," explained Marianne. "We have to have somewhere to take the converts."

Reluctantly, Jo agreed and the next morning found herself bumping through the deserted streets of Brooklyn to 54th Street and Fourth Avenue.

The heat was beginning to reflect off the buildings, as they stood outside waiting for the service to begin. Jo noted that it was not a threatening situation—fellows in blue jeans and long hair sat on the steps reading Scriptures, and girls in peasant dresses quietly praised God. Amazed, she watched as others in carefully pressed suits and short haircuts walked in, praising God in greeting to the hippies. "Some outfit!" Jo murmured.

63

Beyond the freedom and unity found in the service, she was not overly impressed. The preacher had a pronounced English accent, and she found herself looking at the clock more than listening. She could not see why people got so excited about that particular church, but she also found herself wanting to come back, which she did more than once.

Back in Syracuse, Jo spent the summer studying her Bible and books in order to have something to share with the new converts. By this time, her jottings filled many notebooks. Early in August, Sandy, of all people, dropped into the store. Over coffee she explained, "I've left Teen Challenge, and I'm going to Bible school in the fall."

"Bible school? Where?" Jo was interested.

"At Salem—you know, the church you went to with me in Brooklyn. They're starting a school in September, and I need to get it together, so I can teach those we are leading to Christ."

Jo looked wistfully into space. "If only I could afford it. I'd love to join you because I need to do the same thing."

"But you *can* afford it; the tuition is really cheap, because the church looks at it as an outreach. Oh, Jo, you can come," said Sandy excitedly.

"No, I'm in debt, and anyway, who would look after the bookstore?"

The subject was dropped, but God did not drop it; within three days, Jo found herself out of debt and with a replacement for the store. But she was still uncertain. "Who is this Smith guy anyway? I don't know anything about him." The next Sunday she counseled with her pastor and asked whether he had heard of Salem Gospel Tabernacle, or Malcolm Smith.

He shook his head. "Never heard of him, or the church. But I'll check it out for you."

The following Sunday, he called her aside. "We've checked on that Malcolm Smith. He's doing a great work down there and the church has been Spirit-filled for nearly fifty years now. If you go to that school, they will give you the training you're looking for."

And so, during the last week of August, in a borrowed car piled with their few possessions, Jo and Sandy drove into Spanish Harlem and rented a room. They sat on their cases, ate rolls and drank coffee. It was a sticky night, and the reek of garbage and hot pollution came through the open window mingled with the cries, laughter, shouting and cursing of a thousand families within earshot. Jo shuddered and wondered what the next few months would bring.

The next morning was the first day of school, and it came to her that she had not yet asked if she could attend the school! On top of that, everything went wrong. They missed the train, got caught in the middle of rush hour at Times Square, and, blinded by sweat and deafened by the screeching trains, finally emerged from the darkness at 53rd Street on the RR line, at eight thirty.

They were half an hour late, classes had begun, and Jo didn't know if she could join the school. The two raced into the deserted basement of the church. Someone was talking in a Sunday school room in the far corner. On their toes they made their way to the door, planning to slip in and explain later. Sandy turned the latch and pushed, but nothing happened. She tried again, jiggling the latch this time. The voice stopped talking inside. Sandy, red-faced and embarrassed, pushed harder, and the whole wall, now revealed as a partition, shook dangerously.

This was hideous—what an introduction! The door finally burst open to the applause of the class within. Sandy went in, but Jo hung back dreading the eyes of the class. She heard Sandy apologizing, and the next she knew Sandy reached out and dragged her into the class.

She stood clutching her Bible and notebook, her hair in her eyes. "My name is Joanne," she blurted out, "Could I come to your school?"

VII

School settled down to a regular discipline of classes during September and October. As lecture followed lecture the Bible began to come together for the students, and they began to glimpse the overall plan of God. But my great concern was for the hour set aside for simply waiting on God. It was a vital hour. It kept us in tune with God in the middle of our studies, and made those studies part of our walk with Him instead of just a series of facts fed into our minds. Yet it also presented the greatest danger. If we started thinking of it as a "spiritual" meeting other than another area of learning and especially one deliberately planned to save us from dead form, we were in danger of winding up with the worst form of all; a religious act that had no life. If that hour was not a vital interaction between ourselves and God, then we would be sucked into the very professionalism we were so anxious to avoid.

From the beginning, the chapel hour was set for ten fifteen, after two hours of lecture and a coffee break. We sat in two or three rows to be close enough to hear each other in times of sharing. Floyd or I stood out in the front and led the service. We worshiped freely, prayed for specific requests, sang songs, psalms, and praises, and shared testimonies. Usually whoever was leading gave an exhortation. As services go, it was a good meeting, but there was something missing—something vital.

"It is the same element that is missing in the church, only here it is magnified and staring at us," we observed one day as we sat at the counter in the coffee shop. "We just sit there having a meeting. There's no dynamic communication with God anymore." We had come to a dead end. We *were* walking in the glorious light of God's presence and flowing in worship much more than we ever had before, but still there was this tug deep inside. We had to move on, not to something else, but to discover what walking in the light was really all about.

Who are we anyway, I asked, suddenly aware of the question looming inside me and demanding to be answered. Definitely we knew who we were: we were the church, the company of the born-again ones who are His called-out people. We knew that the church was not any one denomination, nor was it a building, but was made up of every person who had been reborn. I had often said, "You cannot go to church—you *are* the church—and when we gather, it is the church coming together."

But who are you, really? *Why* do you have to gather? The question persisted. Why was there so much insistence on *gathering together* in the New Testament? Why not isolated Christians, who knew about each other and occasionally conferred with one another? It occurred to me that I did not know of an isolated Christian in the New Testament. They were always in company with others. The emphasis was so strong that, in the days of the letter to the Hebrews, when to gather together could bring persecution on their

68

heads, they were exhorted not to forsake the assembling of themselves together. I thought of the persecuted Christians in Russia and China who risked their lives to gather together.

Who are we that we must gather together in order to continue in this way called Christianity? Over the years I had learned that when God is about to give an answer to us, He begins by giving the question. God's answers are always staring us in the face but we do not see them unless we are asking the question. And He gives us the key questions to prepare us for receiving the answers. Now I began to grapple with these questions that had presented themselves to me, knowing that when I was enlarged enough within, He could fit His answer into my understanding.

One day, while reading John's first letter, the truth struck like a bolt of lightning.

"But if we walk in the light as He Himself is in the light, *we have fellowship with one another,* and the blood of Jesus His Son cleanses us from all sin." (I John 1:7)

I had read the phrase thousands of times, but it was as if I had never seen it before. It was saying that walking in the light who is God, is expressed in fellowship with other believers. The reason we gathered together was that, in that fellowship, we express our union with God.

Our love for the brethren is the expression of our love union with God in the Spirit. My submission to Jesus as Lord was true only when it included submission to the brethren. To serve God could only be fully expressed in serving the fellowship of believers. And, conversely, God ministered His grace to me *through* the brethren, through their words and through the laying on of their hands. Only when we are forgiven and accepted by the gathering of

69

believers can we know what God's forgiveness actually is. My walk with God was entwined with my walk with other brothers and sisters in the Lord.

This is what was missing! We had set aside an hour to receive from God as if we were all isolated units that had a private line to God. That had been fine as we had begun to walk in the Spirit, but now our frustration was because we had overlooked one vital fact: the enjoyment and growth in fellowship with God was in direct proportion to our fellowship with the brethren.

I began to think about the word fellowship. A man had once defined it to me as "two fellows in one ship." That definition had a lot to commend it. The word for fellowship in the Greek of the New Testament means, "to share together." It was used to describe a business partnership, or the marriage union: it always implied a union where partners give to each other. It was akin to the word covenant, which described the union of two as blood brothers.

The description of the church in the New Testament began to make a lot more sense to me now. We are called the Body of Christ. A body is an orderly arrangement of cells wherein each one interacts with the others for the good of the whole. Every cell, organ, muscle of my body is committed in a selfless giving relationship to the rest of the body. Together in this commitment, the cells of my body had one purpose, which was to manifest *me* to the world. In this orderly arrangement, I was able to be in every part of my body expressed through it how I would.

So—we *are* the Body of Christ! Not isolated Christians struggling alone to do His will and occasionally checking in with each other, but rather members of His Body, vitally united to Him and every other member of the Body. We are incorporated into an arrangement of sharing in our growth and ministering life that we have received from the head.

The hand serves the rest of the body, as do the feet, and every other organ. Not one organ is self-sufficient. The most important is totally dependent on the most insignificant. Together in such a fellowship, we could express the life of Him who dwells in all of us— the Lord Jesus Christ.

This is where the flow of life from the head is. Supposing my hand tried to receive life from the head disregarding the arm and shoulder? Any one member of the Body is incapable of receiving life and ministry from the head, without relying on fellowship with the brothers and sisters around him. The greatest flow of God's glory comes to any individual in the context of the rest of the Body.

This might sound as if individuality could be lost in the community. Actually the reverse is true, for only as I find my place as part of the whole can my individuality be fully expressed. I can only become the unique person I am in company with others.

The New Testament also describes the Church as being like Solomon's Temple, each member a living stone, together resting on the foundation of Jesus Christ and filled with God's glory. One stone looks much like another until placed in a correct relationship with other stones. Then each stone fits into a design and contributes a part of the whole that no other could. The ordinary stone now finds its true and unique purpose, not by laying by itself but by being built into a greater whole.

Participation in such a community of people involves death to independent living. I realized that death to self cannot be defined or expressed merely to God alone; it had to be worked out in the fellowship of believers. Interrelating with the rest of the Body, we would discover exactly what we had died to and how it must be implemented in practical life.

I sat back in my chair to take in all that the Spirit was showing me. My involvement in the Body of Christ over the years had been as an isolationist, an independent. I had never felt that I really needed anyone to help me do God's will, unless I needed them to help work out what I had seen to be God's plan. This word fellowship, dropped into my heart by the Holy Spirit, confronted me with a concept of community where each one recognized that in some way the other was a part of their ministry, where each one needed the other and was not ashamed to say so. Surprisingly, the thought did not threaten me as I would have expected. The breaking that the Spirit had accomplished in me a year before was deeper than I had dreamed, and He was now giving me something in addition to that experience. He had shown me I could not build His Church—only He could. Now He showed me what He meant. He extended His kingdom through His multi-membered Body, and I found the thought exciting me.

Long gone were the days when I would return to show an awestruck congregation the scalps I had collected in the latest evangelistic foray, days when the congregation only looked on while the minister did all the work. We had discovered already to some extent that *we* were the Body of Christ, and what I did, I was enabled to do by the life that flowed from them to me. Any extension of His visible reign that I was involved in was not my victory alone to gloat over but rather to rejoice with the Body, recognizing that though accomplished through me, it was done by *us*—and specifically, Christ in us.

I walked to the door of my office and opened it, pausing to listen to the chapel service in the basement outside. They were sitting in three rows this morning. The front row was looking at Floyd, and the other rows looked at Floyd and the necks of those in the row in front. Even in the togetherness

72

of a meeting, each one was separate and isolated from the other.

In so many churches the congregation had often reminded me of plants in a greenhouse, sitting stiffly looking at the back of someone's head, listening to a preacher answer questions no one was asking. I had seen something similar in Brooklyn. The groups that met in the homes made up of ordinary folk from the neighborhood were so free and informal. Some of those same people, when they came to the services on Sunday, seemed to put on a mask with their Sunday suit. A certain attitude settled over them as they picked up their Bibles and hymn books. By the time they sat in their pews, they were strictly isolated islands. No traffic in or out. Not two fellows in one ship but each man in his own dinghy. Our fellowship in the school was far more free and spontaneous than that, but as I watched them sitting at the front of the basement, I knew we were not experiencing *fellowship*.

In the kitchen I prepared a cup of tea, still listening to the chapel service. They were taking prayer requests, sharing the needs of people broken down with problems they couldn't solve for themselves. The prayers were asking that the Spirit would meet those needs where the people were. I was sure He could, but in the light of what I had seen, those needs should be met by the Spirit ministering *through other believers*. Then what about us? Didn't we have needs, fears, hang-ups and problems? Fellowship should mean that we unmasked ourselves and had brothers pray with us, sharing what God had shown them, and helping us grow in areas where we were having difficulty. Locked up inside this group was a vast deposit of grace, ministries and gifts of the Spirit, but our masks and walls were what kept it locked up.

Fellowship' would demand an unmasked company, an openness to each other, a walking in light where nothing is hidden. I found myself backing away from that. I analyzed my reasons and found that I was afraid of what I had seen in some groups where there was a morbid obsession with problems and a sick desire to confess sins in public. The more sins one had to confess the more spiritual one appeared in the group's eyes. That was a fleshly distortion of what fellowship really meant. I had seen other groups who were demanding that masks be torn off before being specifically so instructed by the Spirit. It meant some were being exposed before they could handle it, and in many cases the self-appointed unmaskers were shocked and embarrassed into silence by what they discovered.

No, I knew that fellowship was simply being honest and walking in the light, not living a life of pretense and cover. Fellowship meant being ready to accept my brother as God accepted him, to love and direct him without feeling superior to him. I would expect exactly the same from him.

But even yet I was afraid of the thought and I had to admit I didn't want anyone to know that sometimes I was fearful, despondent and in need of encouragement. There were areas of my life in which I suffered with many a lonely battle, mainly because I was not willing to admit to anyone I needed help. I knew that God had forgiven me of my past sins, but I had to receive and hear that forgiveness from my brothers and sisters. I, too, was one of the masked people. Walking back to my office, I looked again at the students. We *were* a fellowship, we did love one another, and we were committed to each other as best we knew how. But the Spirit seemed to be pushing us to something far more than we had as yet dreamed of.

But how could we make such a fellowship happen? We couldn't. I knew that only the Holy Spirit could. It was while reading over I John 1:7 again that another word leaped out at me, "We *have* fellowship." To be in fellowship with God is

74

to be in fellowship with my brothers. We didn't have to create it or pray for it—the miracle had happened the day we were born again. What we needed was to have that miraculous bond which was forged by the Spirit to be made manifest. It was not something to be grasped at but rather to be recognized as already there in the Spirit.

I left the matter there for a number of days. I was ready to be involved in fellowship of such a nature and watched and waited for the Holy Spirit to bring it about.

The weekly meetings on the New Jersey side of the city continued with even greater crowds and results. I had found that I did not have to give up the meetings to take on the school; the increased load had been met by increased strength and revelation.

Looking out over the great crowd of eager faces week after week, I realized that this again was not a situation we could describe as fellowship. These people loved each other obviously, but with a love that could not be tested or have any demands laid on it. We only met on one night of the week in a certain kind of atmosphere. The living out of the life, the facing of problems was essentially a solo affair in all the other hours of the week. The kind of love that fellowship spoke of was a tested and tried kind of love. It was Christ's own love in His Body and expressed through the Body. It would be called to costly involvement, sometimes to prolonged patience. It would always be vulnerable. It was a love that saw God at work in a brother beyond the outward appearance of failure. It wasn't that these hundreds of charismatics didn't love each other. This kind of public meeting was just not the place to start learning fellowship.

Such a fellowship could not begin in the larger body at Salem, for that kind of living commitment can only be expressed among a small number of people—those whom we providentially meet and get to know. I remembered the parallel of our bodies to the Body of Christ. My finger has a close commitment to my palm and other fingers that it does not have to the wrist and arm. It *is* committed to the whole body, but only by being first committed to the small circle of members immediately surrounding it. So it is with the Body of Christ. I cannot be involved in fellowship with the universal church—but I *am* in fellowship with that church by being in fellowship with those members with whom I live and walk through life in a very local situation.

Obviously, the Bible school was ideally suited as a place for such a commitment. If we could learn to walk in fellowship, it could spread through us to the whole Body that met in Salem. Then we would truly be a Body, in a two-way covenant; with the Lord and each other. I realized afresh that it was easier to minister to a hall of charismatics than to be involved with a group of people in living fellowship. My mask was never questioned in public, for the people already assumed that I needed no help to live the Christian life, but the public platform was not the place to suddenly take off a mask. Rather, as I took off the mask with those immediate to me, the result would show on the public platform.

VIII

The origins of many great rivers can be traced back to the most insignificant springs. In the same way our fellowship started one grey November morning in a most matter-of-fact way. Whoever it was that made the suggestion did not realize that they were easing us into the next depth of the ongoing river of God. As we came out of the kitchen from a coffee break, someone said, "Let's sit in a circle. I'm tired of rows." No one objected, and so we pulled our chairs into a circle. And, immediately, it felt "right." The worship and singing of praise was richer than we could remember, and the sharing touched a depth of communication that we had been longing for.

The circle didn't create anything, *it simply showed us what we were to each other.* Just by the physical seating arrangement, it forced us to see ourselves as stones of His temple that had a relationship to each other. Now no seating arrangement can *make* a fellowship happen; that miracle was accomplished when the Holy Spirit brought us together into the Body of Christ. The sitting in a circle forced us to physically face each other in the conscious presence of God, and so lead us to face each other in the Spirit and realize who we were to each other as we lived together in Him.

The circle took the focus away from Floyd or myself and made us more aware of the community of the group. Although still the leaders of the group, our being in the circle was a mute testimony to the fact that we were part of the Body and that we needed the ministry that the other members had for us. The students were part of our growth even as we were part of theirs.

Looking each other in the eye helped us to be real with each other. Joys and sorrows reflected in our faces, and it helped us to throw aside the mask and to freely share our needs and triumphs. We began to learn that our victories, shared from yesterday, met someone's need today.

One day I slipped into the basement in the middle of the chapel hour; the group was in prayer and did not notice my approach. Deeply discouraged by problems I could see no way through, I had no desire to participate at all, yet I took a chair on the edge of the circle. I sat aware of my problem, exhausted by it, yet knowing I was sitting in His presence. As a mute I sat before God.

The worship stilled and Chris began to speak in prophecy. Although no living soul knew of my problem, her words spoke instantly to it. As she ceased, another followed, and then yet another. It was like a message being preached, each point taken up by a different person. As the final word came to a triumphant crescendo, we all burst into praise and clapping. I was a new man, my problem solved by the wisdom in the prophecies. God had ministered to me through the Body.

It was a new experience to be involved in each other, and to let Christ's love come through each of us to the others. It was far easier to sit in a row viewing the back of someone's head. Our masks came off as we walked with each other in the light. We didn't pull them off of each other by demanding confession or revelation of the past, nor did we take sick delight in revealing ourselves. In God's providence, we naturally lived honestly with each other.

We soon discovered we were not perfect; indeed, we offended and hurt each other in many small ways. But, because we also learned to forgive one another with God's kind of forgiveness, they are incidents that have long been forgotten. In the old days they might have been held and nursed until they became walls of bitterness and sources of division. However, we didn't learn what forgiveness was overnight.

We soon saw that being channels of God's grace, forgiving and being merciful to each other *was based on what we saw of God, not what we saw in each other.* God loved us not because we deserved it, but because of Himself. He had taken the guilt and hurt of our sin in the person of Jesus, who bore its penalty and poison away. This is the light into which we had come—a clearer understanding of who God is and what He had done. We live in that light and make judgments of each other in that light. We confront each other in the light of who God is, and what He has done and is doing for and in us. If God has already extended grace and forgiveness to me, and to my brothers and sisters, I have no choice but to forgive them and have mercy. To withhold it from them is actually to withhold it from myself.

Some of us grappled with the question of forgetting. To forgive is one thing, but how can I forget? This extended beyond the ways in which we might hurt each other day by day, to the things that we knew or discovered about each other from our past. How could we forget that a man was once in a certain area of sin?

Forgiving as God forgives is to forget as God forgets.

That is, not to have it leave the mind. God is omniscient: there is no item of knowledge that He does not know. When God forgives because of what He has accomplished for us in Christ, He chooses not to bring it to His mind again. We are called to deal with each other in the same way in the light of the same act of God in Christ.

The parable that Jesus told concerning the lost son in Luke 15 shows how God forgives and forgets. The boy, after squandering half a fortune and dragging his father's name in the gutter, returned home asking for forgiveness. But the father had forgiven him from the moment he went away. At the sight of the boy he runs and embraces him, expressing that forgiveness. But that forgiveness must be worked out in such a way that forgetting will happen.

They were still a great way from the farm, and the father, looking at his son's unkempt and ragged clothes, ordered that the best robe be brought and put on him. He is saying by this, that before they arrive at the farm the son is going to be dressed in such a fashion that no one will know the extent of his sin.

Forgiveness is to say to the forgiven, I will not bring this matter up to anyone else. Only you and I will know what you have done.

The boy had prepared a little speech in which he relinquished the right to be called his father's son and asked only to be called a servant. He was content with the servants' quarters if only he could come back. The father had a perfect opportunity to make the son pay for his sin. Every time the son sat and considered his lot in the servants' quarters, each time he looked wistfully at expensive clothes unable to buy them on his servant's pittance, he would bitterly remember his failure and foolishness. Though forgiven, he would pay for his sin forever. The knife of condemnation would always turn in his heart.

Instead, the father gave him his ring. A ring in the society

80

of those days was akin to a credit card bearing the initials of the owner as a guarantee of payment on purchased goods. The boy was reinstated as a son and given his father's credit in the stores. In doing this, the father was removing anything that would bring up the old wound to the boy.

Forgiveness is to say to the forgiven, I will not bring this matter up to you again or remind you of it in any way that would make you suffer.

They arrive home and a great feast is prepared for the homecoming. The elder brother sulks in the barnyard and refuses to come in. The father comes to him, asks a reason why, and receives an angry reply. "After he spends all your money on wild living, you forgive him and throw a feast." It was a perfect opportunity for the father to feel the greatness of his act. What the brother said was true; his act of forgiveness was magnificent, and it had cost a great deal, though love had hardly noticed it. Here was a sympathetic ear that would listen to a rehash of all the younger brother's crimes and enable the father to gloat over the fact of having forgiven the boy. He could have used his forgiveness to gain the reputation of a saint. Instead he gently rebuked the older son and said, "But we had to be merry and rejoice, for this brother of yours was dead and has begun to live, and was lost and has been found." He plainly states that there was to be no further conversation. Whatever the boy had done was a closed book and the father refused to talk about it.

Forgiveness is the solemn promise to the forgiven that the matter will never be raised to be gloated over. You promise to consider it as dead.

This is how God has forgiven us—He, by the finished work of Christ, refuses to bring our sins to mind. He does not bring them up to torment us, nor does He disclose them to the church. Fellowship with God is in this context. I know

81

He knows the worst about me, but He loves me and accepts me as if I had never sinned. Our fellowship with one another is based on the same bloodshedding of Jesus Christ. It is in knowing what we were that we accept each other as God accepts us, and we forget as God forgets.

It is this that is expressed in Ephesians 4:31-5:2.

Let all bitterness and wrath and anger and clamor and slander be put away from you, along with all malice. And be kind to one another, tender-hearted, forgiving each other, just as God in Christ also has forgiven you. Therefore be imitators of God, as beloved children; and walk in love, just as Christ also loved you, and gave Himself up for us, an offering and a sacrifice to God as a fragrant aroma:

and Colossians 3:12-14.

And so, as those who have been chosen of God, holy and beloved, put on a heart of compassion, kindness, humility, gentleness and patience; bearing with one another, and forgiving each other, whoever has a complaint against any one; just as the Lord forgave you, so also should you. And beyond all these things put on love, which is the perfect bond of unity.

It is not only a matter of giving forgiveness but also of taking it, daring to believe not only the love that God has toward us but also to receive that love in the embrace of fellowship.

But we learned that there is more to walking in the light with each other than forgiveness. Our life is an ongoing maturity in God, not only a putting behind of the past. We are part of one another's growth in God. We helped each other grow by teaching how the mistakes that gave rise to the need of forgiveness would not be repeated again. It was a costly love to tell another what was wrong and point out how to overcome, costly because it might not be received. It faced us with the reality of the fellowship when we accepted what another was sharing.

The most important factor in our growth together was learning to see Christ in each other and trust Him there, believing that He who had begun a good work would perform it till the day of Jesus Christ. To encourage one another to work out salvation with fear and trembling because we were convinced that it was God who was at work in us, willing and doing of His good pleasure. When love is flowing between persons, faith is also at work, for faith works by love. We reached out and picked each other up with encouragement, believing that the Life who was within the stumbling brother would accomplish His work and nothing could stop Him.

We all exercise a shadow of this kind of faith—love on a natural level. The mother takes baby and sets it on its feet, while anxious father awaits it at the other side of the room. The baby is told to "walk to Daddy." To an ignorant observer that is the moment of the ridiculous, for in the first place the child does not understand the term "walk" and also it is obvious that the leg muscles are so weak and unresponsive that the child cannot walk to Daddy or anyone else. To a casual beholder, the child was obviously born to crawl. The child falls down the moment the mother lets go, but the process is repeated again and again for weeks, and gradually the child walks.

Why such perseverance? *Faith which worked by love.* Faith in the human life in the child that predictably would stand erect on two legs. Unshakable faith in that life, coupled with love that gave endless patience, eventually matured the crawling babe to a little walking human.

As a group of Christians we had lots of falls and tumbles, but we learned to believe in Christ who was in us that He would undoubtedly walk His life through us.

Jesus exercised this kind of faith in His Father's plan when He called Simon by the new name of Peter, a name which meant *a stone*. "Stone" hardly described that man who constantly moved and shifted. Jesus began calling him by the name that would describe him when He had finished with him. He did not see him as he now was, but as he would be. When he acted like his Simon nature in denying the Lord, Jesus' response was, "Go and tell my disciples *and Peter*." Not only a message that he was still a disciple, but also that Jesus still saw him as the finished product.

Through the fall and winter months, we learned to call each other by our Peter names, to see each other not as we were but as we would be when the Spirit had finished with us. In this way we not only helped each other leave behind our past, but also to move on to His glorious future.

None of this happened in a day! Gradually we became more confident in walking in the light together, discovering what fellowship really was and becoming aware of a deep committed love being forged between us.

IX

"Joanne, you're wrong! I am not a shepherd, and I never will be!" My words were clipped, angry and stinging. Jo looked back wide-eyed from behind her glasses. Several of us had been drinking coffee in the kitchen during a break between classes, and in the course of conversation she had said, a smile flickering at the corners of her mouth, "I am your sheep, and you are my shepherd." They were words thrown out lightly in relation to something else altogether, but somehow they had threatened me and brought out the blistering response. Like the echo of a slap, they seemed to hang in air between us in the lenghtening silence that followed. I would have given anything to recall them, and tried to think of something to say to take away the sting but nothing would come.

Jo broke through the wall of hurt, tears brimming in her eyes. "It's not only me," she stammered. "We all think of you like that. We know you're very human and that you fail, but we have come to know Jesus through your life and the truth you have shared. I know He has a lot more to say through you. It doesn't matter what you say, God has given you to me to be my shepherd."

Murmuring something about being sorry, and avoiding looking at her eyes, I shook my head and went to my office. What had made me lash out like that? I didn't have to ask; it was the idea of her, and the others, following me as a shepherd. And just at the thought, my original horror at the idea came flooding back. The evolution of the idea of teaching a small group of students had satisfied my orignal discovery of what a disciple was. We had deliberately called them students, to avoid the idea of disciples. Student was a nice, safe word that I could live with, but the idea of someone being apprenticed to me in the Christian life was something I could not swallow. I shied away from the very idea. Who was I—or anyone else for that matter— to start telling others to make me their example of Christianity. I comforted myself with the words of an old saint who, in the beginning of my Christian walk, had told me not to get my eyes on him or to follow him, but to keep my eyes on the Lord. Students who attended my lectures and learned truth, I could enjoy, but I couldn't apprentice them to the actual living of it, as they saw it in me. They had to keep their eyes on the Lord, not me.

I had heard of so-called "discipleship groups" that had sprung up across the East. I had found that they were usually headed by one strong personality who bore down on the members of the group, demanded total submission, blind obedience and the carrying out of his every whim. Whenever I heard about such groups, I dismissed them with a shrug. "That's dicatorship, not discipleship—Hitler, dressed in lamb's wool." I knew what discipleship *wasn't*, but I had never faced up to what true discipleship *was*. Because of this, I wouldn't even use the name *disciple*. No, *student* was a word that kept a nice, safe distance between me and them in the practicing of truth in life.

But now the outburst in the kitchen had brought me face to face with the fact that the issue was not resolved. The call to make disciples kept intruding, but I could not see how I could ever accept it.

The pressure had been building from another direction during the previous weeks. With the publication of the book, *Turn Your Back On the Problem,* and a number of Bible studies I had given, came more and more invitations to preach. I was turning them down because of my commitment to the church and the Bible school students. Things had finally come to a head a few days previously when a prominent figure in an historic denomination asked me to address a gathering of his ministers on the Baptism in the Holy Spirit. As was my policy, I refused because it conflicted with the school schedule and also a service in the church.

He became red in the face, his words short: "That's right, go back and teach your Brooklyn sheep! They are fat, sleek and well-combed. Let the starving masses go unfed—but remember *they* have no shepherd at all." He turned on his heel and walked away. Upon reflection, I found myself agreeing with the essence of what he was saying. And the more I thought about it the more frustrated I became.

And it was this and all the rest of it that was behind the outburst at Joanne's innocent remark. And since it had come to that, I knew I had to make a decision. I would follow my heart which reached out to the masses of sheep without a shepherd. I would keep my commitment to the students and train them, but after that, move out into the great field of the renewal of the Spirit in the church at large.

I sat with Floyd and talked it all through. He was doubtful and suggested we share it with the elders and see how they felt. I agreed, counting on God's will being revealed in counsel with other brothers. The elders were unimpressed with the idea. They sat around the walls of my office almost unaware of me, talking among themselves of our ministry in the church, and the Bible school, eulogizing the students who were living a life of freedom in grace that was an example before the rest of the congregation. I heard them: I should stay on as pastor . . . give some time to the renewal movement . . . the work was really with the students.

I looked at them, hearing their conversation drift in and out of my racing thoughts. How can these men tell me what to do? While ten thousand hungry Spirit-filled people sit out there, waiting to be fed, longing to be given content to their experience, these men sit and discuss what a wonderful church we have, along with the need of a visit to Mrs. Jones. Dear God, have these men ever seen what I have seen? Have they ever stood before a thousand hungry eyes, waiting for the truth that is burning to be given? Have they ever felt the flow of the Spirit giving words and sentences, that pours light into confused minds? Have they ever stood carried on the ascending praise that spontaneously broke out when truth was seen? And they are the ones deciding that I should come back and feed and re-feed the fat, sleek sheep.

What was the use. I clenched and unclenched my hands under the desk, furious that I had decided to submit to the counsel of my elders, and not trusting God in them at all. They did not see it from my perspective. Added to the frustration, I kept hearing Joanne say, "I am your sheep and you are my shepherd." No, I am not. God had given me a teaching ministry to the masses. What was the point of giving up what I knew God had given me to do, in order to engage in what I could not do?

Mentally I drifted in and out of the meeting, and was

thankful to get home to the inky silence of the bedroom, punctuated only by Jean's steady breathing, and the muffled sound of Donna turbulently reliving some crisis of the day.

Suddenly, I remembered: in three days we were going to Puerto Rico. *Three days!* In all the discussion, I had forgotten. Jack Swift, a close friend who was a realtor in Brooklyn, had asked Jean and I to accept this all-expenses paid trip that he and his wife Linda wanted to give us, as a love offering to the Lord. Gratefully we accepted, and looked forward to getting away from the remnants of winter and the chill winds of Brooklyn to the hot sands and palms of the Caribbean.

My mind wandered back to the last time we had gone to the Virgin Islands, three years before, and there heard God speak the words, *I will build my church.* I remembered the torment in which we had gone and began to praise God. *That* had been darkness, *this* was a momentary hassle on the road of light. I was settled in my heart that He was building His church, with or without me. My only concern at this point was that I continued to flow along in the river of His purpose. With God revealed to us in Jesus Christ, who could miss that purpose? I rested in Him, turned over and fell into a dreamless sleep.

Puerto Rico was everything we needed—hotel on the beach, tropical fruit, coconut milk under the palms, and the sun-drenched sand where we lay for most of the day.

The fine white sand was hot under me as I lay letting it pour through my fingers. We drank in the deep penetrating heat of the sun, the gentle breeze stirring the palms above us and the mini-waves that played on the shore. We let them soothe and unravel the knots of tension. I silently thanked God that once again He had taken me over one thousand miles to get me to stay still long enough to relax.

The command of Psalm 46:10, "Cease striving and know that I am God" is the first law of the spiritual life. We must be still from our own striving and hear God speaking. I yawned and stretched. If He was going to speak to me on these sands, I was ready to hear.

It was on the third day, coming into the foyer of the hotel, that we were surprised to see Peter Noonan, waiting on line for a room, and his wife Ruth, sitting on a case. Peter was the chairman of our board of deacons, and was the last person we expected to see in the foyer of our hotel.

We were further stunned when Ruth came over to us and confided that Peter had come to share with me what he felt the Lord was saying. *Peter Noonan and Ruth—coming all the way to Puerto Rico to tell me what the Lord had said? Unreal!* They were too solid for that. They knew better than that, surely! They had been taught from when they first came to Christ, that prophecy *confirms* not directs. What kind of nonsense was this? What possessed them?

Ruth had been born in Puerto Rico and was a true Latin, wearing her feelings on her sleeve and face. She looked earnestly at me, as she told us quietly, "You know, it's got to be heavy on Peter's heart, or he would never have come." I nodded slowly, wondering what the next hours held.

The next morning after breakfast, the four of us lay on the white beach, comfortable before the sun got too high. Peter began to share what was on his heart. He had heard of my restlessness to go and teach masses, and as he had thought about it, he knew he had to share what he saw. His words were soft spoken but intense. "You are to stay in the church, Malcolm. It's to be a model to the renewal movement of what fellowship really is—and the school is somehow at the core of it all. Those students are your disciples; through them you will touch the world." There was that word again. All these months it had lain hidden beneath the word student, and now Peter had put them together and it had risen to confront me. Not just students, but apprentices that needed on-the-job training. Dear God, why did they have to come and disturb this paradise with the question?

Taking a deep breath and waiting a moment before speaking, I gently tried to share the thoughts I had when talking with the elders. I spoke of the great renewal movement in which I had providentially been given an open door to teach. "But where are you leading them?" asked Peter. "Just to more meetings to get blessed? You know there is more to the Christian walk than that, you've taught us too well. All you are doing is prolonging their dilemma! They have got to come to discover fellowship and living in a commitment to each other." I shifted uncomfortably in my beach chair. That was true. Meeting in an auditorium once a week was not church—just a random gathering of Christians. And there was so much more I could not share outside of a church of Spirit-filled people.

"And what about New Year's eve eighteen months ago?" Peter went on. "I thought you said that the Lord told you to make disciples. All you are doing is making blessing-seekers, if you leave off the work in the school." I had forgotten that I had shared that night ride up Fourth Avenue, and wished I had never mentioned it.

He sat back in his chair. "You *know* that what I am saying *is* true: this *is* a confirmation. You are anchored to Brooklyn, however many others you may teach. You are anchored to the disciples in the Bible school."

We sat silently. The waves washed below us, and a voice shouted in the distance in Spanish. He was trying to sell coconuts. I knew there was truth in what Peter said, but rather than just say words, I remained silent. It came together in something Jean and I had seen the previous day.

91

We had gone on a tour of the rain forest, and on the way had stopped in a small shack at the side of the road to watch a Puerto Rican craftsman make pottery. Taking a handful of wet clay, he had flung it onto his rapidly spinning wheel. Putting his hands around it, he seemed to discover a pot and pulled it out of the clay. The shapeless mass was there no more, but a vase was happening in front of my eyes. I was excited at the genius of his hands and ease of movement. The vase spun around smoothly. Plunging his hands inside he shaped the inner part of the piece of art. He stood back. Magnificent. Then he had taken some small sharp tools and carefully applied them to the clay. I felt myself tighten up. Surely the sharp instruments would gouge the fragile side of the vase. It was running so smoothly, this was such a risk to take. Instead he applied only the pressure that was needed to bring about an intricate design on the pot that was carved into its smooth sides.

The sight had left a deep impression on me, now it came vividly back to me almost as a word from the Lord. The Holy Spirit had taken me —a mass of clay—with no shape or direction and brought me into the flow of the Spirit. He had fashioned and pressured me and a ministry had happened under His hands. He had plunged His hand inside me and worked His will in the depths. I was secure in Him and used to His smooth flow through me. Now, in the last weeks, all had been upset. Words had been spoken that cut against the smooth flow of the teaching ministry. First the words spoken in my spirit on Fourth Avenue, then Ray's demand that he be my disciple, then Jo, most recently the elders, and now Peter. They all said the same thing, and as I had looked at them, they seemed to be aimed at destroying the smooth comfortable flow of the Spirit, and that had annoyed and threatened me.

Now I saw clearly that they were sharp instruments in the

hands of the master potter, the genius of creation, who was using them to trace His design into my life. Not to stop the smooth flow of the Spirit but to introduce an intricate, detailed pattern within it. I still couldn't reconcile the idea of me apprenticing anyone to the living of the Christian life; I still did not think of Joanne, or anyone else, as my sheep. But I was at rest, and I knew it would only be a matter of time before the pattern that He was etching into my life emerged out of the pressure of the sharp, annoying words.

I thanked Peter for his obedience, and praised God for the way His church works. For the next couple of days we plunged into enjoying the island under the expert guidance of Ruth. Tanned, refreshed and excited, we landed back in Kennedy to a grey drizzle.

X

Beethoven's Ninth Symphony filled the living room and covered the sounds of children playing stickball in the street outside. Jean had taken our children to buy spring clothes on nearby 86th Street, and I was alone in the house. My attention was on the symphony, yet at the same time I was looking over Paul's letters to the Thessalonians.

My eyes scanned the lines, and I was about to turn to something else, when suddenly a paragraph at the end of the second letter arrested my attention.

For you yourselves know how you ought to follow our example, because we did not act in an undisciplined manner among you, nor did we eat anyone's bread without paying for it, but with labor and hardship we kept working night and day so that we might not be a burden to any of you; not because we do not have the right to this, but in order to offer ourselves as a model for you, that you might follow our example. For even when we were with you, we used to give you this order: If anyone will not work, neither let him eat. (II Thess. 3:7-10)

I must have read that a hundred times before, yet I was hearing it for the first time. The words seemed to stand out on the page shocking and exciting me at the same time. Rereading them aloud, my suspicion was confirmed: he *was* saying what I had heard. *He was deliberately setting himself up as an example of the way the Christian life should be practiced.*

Following the cross references, I saw that I had already passed over this thought within the last half hour and missed it. In I Thess. 1:6 he wrote: "You also became imitators of us and of the Lord, having received the word in much tribulation with the joy of the Holy Spirit." And he also expected *his* converts to be models or examples to *their* converts—"so that you became an example to all the believers in Macedonia and in Achaia" (I Thess. 1:7).

I turned down Beethoven's Ninth, and continued to follow up the references. To the Philippians, Paul wrote reminding them not only of his verbal teaching but also of that teaching demonstrated in his own life. And he called upon them to do as they had seen him do. "The things you have learned and received and heard and seen in me, practice these things; and the God of peace shall be with you" (Phil. 4:9).

A new body of truth was emerging out of the Scripture before my eyes. To Paul, teaching was never a matter of speaking only, but of modeling that teaching in his life to show new believers exactly how it worked out in practice. This had been the battleground in my mind for months. Now, as I heard the truth from Scripture, I was aware that a surrender to it had already taken place deep within me, and a new spring of life was bubbling up.

But, I argued with myself, how could Paul call on people to look up to him, and follow his example? Surely Jesus is the only example! It would have been bad enough if they had followed his example *against* his wishes. But in these paragraphs he was admitting that he had consciously intended that they would model their lives after his. All I had been taught for years was saying that this was unthinkable. *Unthinkable.* Yet, the thought persisted. If he laid plans for new believers to model themselves after his example, was that not an indication that this was his methodology in establishing converts in the faith?

The idea took fire within. I recalled a meeting I had been in a few nights before. At the end of my message the pastor had called those desiring to express their new faith in Christ to come forward. And they had come—shaggy teenagers, businessmen and housewives. Counselors spoke with them and prayed. I watched as they prayed, too, expressing their faith in words, confessing that Jesus was Lord. The counselors handed each one a little book, The Gospel of John, and the newborn babes in Christ walked back up the aisle clutching the book, the doorway to the life they had now come into.

But I could surmise what would happen when they read the Gospel: they would not understand it. Even the magnificent but now archaic language, would seem almost foreign to most of them. Perhaps a number of them would eventually seek out a Bible, stumble onto the Epistles and read of a life style that, to all they had ever known, would be as remote as the far side of the moon. Many of them would live in frustration for months as they pieced it together, and others without any encouragement would simply give up. But wasn't the Spirit of God able to show them the way to live victoriously in Christ? Of course He was! "Then why doesn't He?" the whisper came.

Now He placed the answer in my hand. He had chosen to work primarily through humans, in whom He had come to dwell. If those humans avoided their responsibility, then His work took that much longer. I was shocked at my own thinking, but the verses in front of me, like a river of revelation at the first thaw of spring, flowed irresistibly through the frozen corners of my mind. The early church had not placed a Gospel or Bible in anyone's hands—there was none to give nor would one be published for the masses for fourteen centuries! Then how did the early teachers instruct new born converts? They urged them to observe how they themselves lived out Christ and to follow their example. The babe in Christ had a flesh and blood demonstration of what the Christian life was all about.

A very strong and demanding truth was forming in my mind, one that would convict many and anger many more. We who had been given the responsibility of bringing new converts to maturity had used the Scripture as a means of avoiding that responsibility. That responsibility ultimately carried with it the charge to make disciples. We had said: let the Scriptures make disciples. The Scriptures are the Word of God, but that Word must be seen and demonstrated in lives, if disciples are going to result from it. A living, normal, human example is needed to bring the life set out in Scripture into our normal mundane frame of reference and show not only that it *can* be lived, but how. If we were truly *living Christ* we would be able to take the believer to the Scripture and say, look, this is what's happening here.

All my previous study as to what discipleship was came rushing back to me. It was an apprenticeship kind of learning, the new student taught by the craftsman in a practical on-the-job kind of training situation. The old saint back in my home town of Southend in England came to mind again. I had asked in my naivety to be apprenticed, not specifically

97

to that saint but to the "how" of resting in Christ as he obviously did, the "how" of living Christ in the world. He had pushed me away and told me to keep my eyes on the Lord. I was hurt. My eyes had never been off the Lord! I had wanted a model, a master at living Christ to teach me how to live this life portrayed in Scripture.

Now I saw that this is what Paul had given the Thessalonians. He was not saying he was the perfect man, therefore they should follow him. His letters made it plain that Christ, and only Christ, was the All in All. Paul was saying that Christ living in a believer was an observable fact, and that new believers could learn by observing more mature believers. Paul spoke of a Lord who could be practically followed—and lived—with the help of the lives of those gone before.

That which had been a spring of life within me now leaped boldly, laughing in my spirit, sending my doubts scurrying in disarray and confusion. I laughed at my fleeing doubts, "Are you so shocked that what Paul preached actually *worked*? Are you horrified that Paul expected Christ to be seen in him? Much of what you call humility is a form of religious pride!"

For years I had studied what Paul proclaimed as the Good News, and in the last two years, much of my earlier study which had been dead knowledge, had leaped into life. I now saw clearly that if what Paul stated in the Epistles, and what I was preaching across the land was workable, it would inevitably end up with such a conclusion as this.

To the natural man the Christianity that fills the pages of the New Testament may well be described as the impossible life style. The Gospels tell the history of Jesus Christ in His incarnation, sinless life, death on a cross, resurrection and exaltation. The letters of Paul, Peter, James and John proclaim that history as the legal basis and dynamic source for man's salvation. God grants us His righteousness by causing our sin to be laid upon Jesus, by punishing Him in our place and then having put away that sin forever, raising Him from the dead. A man is declared righteous when he rests in what was done for him in Christ. He knows that God, through Jesus Christ, has pronounced him clean. His sins and iniquities will be remembered no more.

Nor is that all. In the exaltation of Jesus, the Holy Spirit was now His to give to those who would believe. Not only is a man declared righteous through Jesus, but the Spirit comes into Him bringing him rebirth, a union between that Spirit of Christ and the spirit of man. It means that the life of Jesus can be reproduced in us by His Spirit so much so that Paul could say, "Christ lives in me." The Good News is not a call to imitate Jesus, to struggle to be like Him, but rather to let the Holy Spirit live in us and express through us His impossible life style.

Paul wrote it over and over: "Test yourselves to see if you are in the faith; examine yourselves! Or do you not recognize this about yourselves, that Jesus Christ is in you— unless indeed you fail the test?" (II Cor. 13:5) . . . "I have been crucified with Christ; and it is no longer I who live, but Christ lives in me; and the life which I now live in the flesh I live by faith in the Son of God, who loved me, and delivered Himself up for me" (Gal. 2:20) . . . "But the one who joins himself to the Lord is one spirit with Him" (I Cor. 6:17).

This is what makes it good news—and bad news to the man who is proud of his efforts to be like Jesus. Only the man who knows he is bankrupt will turn from all his struggles and helplessly look to God to declare him righteous, and place His Spirit within him. The believer is one who is abandoned to God's work on his behalf in the bloodshedding of Jesus and the giving of the Spirit, believing that He will reproduce the life of His Son in us. For the life is not the fruit of our struggles but the fruit of the Spirit.

I was challenged by the obvious implications of this truth: *if Christ lived in us and expressed Himself through our actions, then He could be seen in a human life.* In fact, to teach such a Gospel *without* demonstrating it tended to make it seem little more than a magnificent theory.

I slumped back in the couch where I had been sitting. The stream of understanding that had come from those verses had ceased, and I knew I would never be the same. I sat in the full light of the Word of God that now bathed my mind and understanding—light that gently hurt and yet was life at the same time. When God's word comes it makes us willing in the day of its power. *I had been wrong.* God had sent me a few fellows and girls to disciple. He had gathered them around me to be apprenticed to life in Christ, and I had missed it. And not just missed it, but so recently pushed one of them away, saying that I was not her shepherd.

In great enthusiasm I had gone after the crowds, the masses. Did I love the crowds, because of the thrill I received in ministering to them? That was not altogether true, but I sensed that there was enough truth in it that when it came to giving myself to one person, and ministering to him with *costly* love—love that was going to cost me time and inconvenience and could possibly get someone angry at me—I was always too busy. *I hadn't been able to see a person; there was a crowd in the way.*

The school was already half over now, and I had missed the joy of cooperating with the Holy Spirit in discipleship. I had spent the time hiding behind the word "student." Yet, had it not happened *without* my cooperation? Had they not followed the way the Spirit expressed Christ through me?

100

Was this not the reason Ray had grown so quickly? The Spirit had used me as a model of what He was teaching Ray whether I liked it or not. What a truth! What a sobering thought! Every Christian was a model of the Christian life, whether they knew it, liked it or not.

I had been wrong. I thanked the Lord then, for showing me just *how* wrong, and asked His forgiveness. And I gave Him my will, no strings attached, and somehow I knew I would never be the same again. The blood of Jesus cleansed from all sin, and I knew the Spirit was now free to work His will in my life. I leaned back, light and alive, to enjoy the Beethoven that still played on.

For the next few days I was absorbed in pursuing the subject and found more and more evidence that this was the way the New Testament Christians worked out Jesus' command to make disciples. Before this, I had always imagined Paul as addressing multitudes. Now he began to emerge from the pages of the Acts and Letters as a man given to individuals. For example, the emphasis on the people who traveled *with* Paul amazed me. The long lists of names at the end of the letters, and the list of those who accompanied him to Jerusalem in Acts 20:4 had never meant anything to me, but now I was beginning to see what they indicated. Here was no isolationist emerging from solitude to address an audience, but one whose private life was open to all. These men who traveled with him to Jerusalem did not appear to have anything in particular to do except be with him. In the light of the Thessalonian letters, it could be assumed that they were with him to learn how normally Christ could live in the life of the man who wrote Galatians 2:20 and Colossians 3:1.

It was no easy task for Paul, and the more I thought about

it, the more I realized what it must have cost him. The first Thessalonian letter hinted at the way he gave himself without reserve that they may come to maturity:

But we proved to be gentle among you, as a nursing mother tenderly cares for her own children. Having thus a fond affection for you, we were well pleased to impart to you not only the gospel but also our own lives, because you had become very dear to us. For you recall, brethren, our labor and hardship, how working night and day so as not to be a burden to any of you, we proclaimed to you the gospel of God. You are witnesses, and so is God, how devoutly and uprightly and blamelessly we behaved toward you believers; just as you know how we were exhorting and encouraging and imploring each one of you as a father would his own children, so that you may walk in a manner worthy of the God who calls you into His own kingdom and glory. (I Thess. 2:7-12)

This was no cold lecture to students, but a deep involvement in the life of those God had given him! Not just a proclaiming of truth, but a demonstration of it by a man who poured his life out for that purpose. "This is salvation come full circle," I mused. Eternal selfless love became flesh, and gave Himself for us, and through His Spirit, that selfless love was shed abroad in our hearts to give us away to others that they might drink of the Water of Life through us. We ate of Jesus, and now others eat of Him through our lives.

Floyd and I were sitting in Tiffany Diner a few mornings later having coffee with Osborne Arnes, a pastor from Staten Island, who lectured in the school. The previous Sunday, the students had ministered in his church, and he was sharing with us what it had meant to the congregation. "You have something to be proud of in God in that dark-haired one, Ray." He paused, "Malcolm, he's your Timothy. It was a joy to hear him."

I smiled weakly. *He's your Timothy.* The words stuck in my mind, and I went home to take another look at what Timothy was to Paul. Paul had probably won him to Christ while in Lystra, and later had had him travel with him. During the early years, they had traveled together, Paul had discipled him, and now he reminded Timothy of how it was done. "But you followed my teaching, conduct, purpose, faith, patience, love, perseverance, persecutions, sufferings, such as happened to me at Antioch, at Iconium and at Lystra; what persecutions I endured and out of them all the Lord delivered me!" (II Tim. 3:10, 11).

The life of God's Spirit had come to Timothy so directly through Paul, that Paul called him, "my true child in the faith" and again, "my beloved son." And it was Paul's last command to Timothy, that he should now do the same to others, who would, in turn, do the same again. "And the things which you have heard from me in the presence of many witnesses, these entrust to faithful men, who will be able to teach others also" (II Tim. 2:2).

Jesus had discipled the twelve, and then sent them to do the same. I had never been so forcibly struck by the Gospels' emphasis on Jesus working with *individuals*. He addressed the multitudes, wept over them, and spent days with them, but the main thrust of His ministry was to give Himself completely to a circle of seventy, to a smaller circle of twelve within which Peter, James, and John were an even smaller circle, reducing maybe to one, for John was the one loved and trained in a special way. When God became flesh, He gave Himself to training a handful of men by word and practical example. When He left them, He told them to go and do the same thing with others. It had been those words that had come to me and thrilled me these long months ago, and only now was I willing for the involvement. From now on while continuing to minister to large gatherings, the main thrust of my ministry would be to those He providentially placed in my path.

In this way leaders would always be emerging from the larger Body of Christ, who, in turn, could model the Christian life before others, on and on in an endless chain. Then we would have what Isaiah had long ago prophesied: "Behold, a king will reign righteously, and princes will rule justly. And each will be like a refuge from the winds, and a shelter from the storm, like streams of water in a dry country, like the shade of a huge rock in a parched land" (Isa. 32:1, 2).

I had never seen it in this light before, but now it was as clear as day. Jesus reigned and we reigned with Him, princes of His kingdom. The new believer who comes into the kingdom, tossed by every wind of doctrine, weary and dry, finds in the princes the shade, the refuge and rivers of water that flow through them from the King. Then our churches would no longer be hospitals and sick bays for crippled Christians but . . . "Then the eyes of those who see will not be blinded, and the ears of those who hear will listen. And the mind of the hasty will discern the truth, and the tongue of the stammerers will hasten to speak clearly" (Isa. 32:3, 4).

XI

My first impulse was to structure a discipleship program, but that was instantly dismissed. Would I never learn that He, who is within us to *will,* is also in us to *do His will?* He not only *tells* us what to do but also, *He is His method of doing it.* I was beginning to learn over the months to wait and discover how He would do what He was telling me.

The church has long heard the command to extend the kingdom of God on earth, to go into all the world and proclaim the Gospel. Most of us who heard neglected to stop and see *how* that was to be done. We rushed off across the world, spending millions of dollars on how *we* thought it should be accomplished. What was Jesus' method in apprenticing twelve men who were to establish the kingdom in the lives of the multitudes? How did the Messiah King train the princes who would be co-rulers in that kingdom? If we could discover His method of making disciples, we would be saved all the grief and heartache that inevitably come from doing things our way. I began to reread the Gospels to see if I could frame the answer.

The familiar story opened up as I read. Here were men from every walk of life, called to follow Him and be part of that inner circle of His apprentices. I saw how unusual the story actually was and how our familiarity with it many times obscures what is really there.

These men did not enroll in seminary, were not called to a course of religious instruction, did not, in fact, attend religious meetings as a part of their training. While rabbis taught their disciples within the temple porches, Jesus had these untrained men with Him out in the market place and in the fields. They did not take part, but watched and listened along with the rest of the multitudes. After the crowds had gone, Jesus would share with them in greater depth the meaning of His words.

The schools of the Pharisees met at regular hours in classrooms, but this One had the whole of life as His classroom. They were walking along the dusty roads of Samaria, or through a village in Galilee when teaching was given they would never forget. He used the details of their lives to apprentice them to their work in the coming kingdom, of fishing for men. They went out to social gatherings together, sometimes the wedding of a friend, sometimes to dine with a critical religious leader, or a curious rich man, and wherever they could share the company of those marked out by the Pharisees and Sadducees as the especially sinful, despised for their reputation as sinners. From those banqueting tables of rich, criminal and religious, He gave His lectures, spontaneously as the circumstance of the moment suggested. At other times they joined the psalm-singing caravans of peasants on their way to the feasts in Jerusalem. His words, spoken informally, became the foundation of the kingdom.

Towards the end of John's Gospel, He said, "As the Father has sent Me, I also send you." But I still didn't know *how* the Father had sent Him. His course of instruction seemed to have no beginning and meandered its way with neither plan nor method until the Ascension. By that time, they had apparently learned all they were intended to, and, from here on *they* were His plan to establish His kingdom in the world.

If there was no plan, it was rather pointless that He should say that we should *go as He had.* It was also ridiculous to think of the all-wise God being incarnate without a plan in the forming of the lives of the princes in the kingdom. I thumbed through the Gospels again. There *had* to be a plan somewhere. Then I read Mark 3:14, "And He appointed twelve, that they might be with Him, and that He might send them out to preach," and I saw with sudden clarity that there *was* a plan, but so unlike anything we had been accustomed to in our evangelistic programs that I had missed it.

The plan was that they should be *with* Him. The Gospel narrative is not so much of how or what He taught, as how He gave Himself to them. He was not only the teacher, He was the teaching. They had to be with Him for He was not teaching them about love, wisdom, truth or humility; He *was* the truth, the love. *He* was the message, the final Word from God in our flesh.

So *with* them, He lived *before* them truth, the living model of His teaching. All He said was demonstrated before them, available to them in His human life. They would observe Him under every conceivable situation, joy or sorrow, challenge or emergency, whatever the Father's providential arrangement of circumstances sent their way.

They did not learn a specific ethic or doctrine. Rather, they scrutinized a life. Christianity is not another religion sharing the stage with all the other philosophies and world religions that offer an ethic. Religions of the world may use some of the same words as Christianity, but they are a Grand Canyon removed.

God's final unveiling of Himself was in the authentic man, Jesus Christ. He is God's complete word of love to this planet. He is what Christians call the Way, not a textbook but a Person. This thought put a lot of things together for me. I realized that the events of the last year and a half had been bringing this fact into focus. I had always preached the Bible, but I had been presenting more a textbook of the good life than a living Jesus. I had concentrated more on a list of positives and negatives than the spirit of life in Christ Jesus. Now I saw what had happened: the content of my message had gradually returned to the Good News Himself, Jesus Christ.

They had to be with Him, because He was the life. These men were apprenticed to life Himself. In His authentic human life, they saw how that life was lived on our human plane. "What was from the beginning, what we have heard, what we have seen with our eyes, what we beheld and our hands handled, concerning the Word of Life—and the life was manifested, and we have seen and bear witness and proclaim to you the eternal life" (I John 1:1, 2).

Jesus was not a man with an unusual amount of love, who gave some of the world's greatest teaching on it. He is what we mean by love, for He is God, being Himself within the confines of our humanity. The Christian can never define love in the abstract, for it has been forever defined in Him. It is the way Jesus of Nazareth was and is. Love is the way He acted and reacted. In being Himself, love was publicly demonstrated.

The twelve beheld that love, and how it was expressed in the tangible decisions and choices that He made. They were watching as love was worked out at their level of existence, even when faced with men plotting with hatred to quench it. In Him they did not see a man with an unusual amount of patience. He was God's infinite patience expressed in our humanity, looking at life through a human mind. Eternal patience was worked out at the human level on earth.

Forgiveness was not an abstract idea. In Jesus they had watched a kind of forgiveness that knew no end, given to enemies and those who did not wish to receive it. They finally realized that it is the way God gives of Himself on behalf of His enemies. Forgiveness was forever written in the blood He shed. Never again could they argue over a fine point of ethics, as to whether or not forgiveness should be given to an individual; they had seen God die for them in Jesus Christ. "Forgive them, Father, for they know not what they do," He had said with iron spikes driven through His hands and feet. In Him, they saw that forgiveness was at the center of the universe.

He didn't give them lectures on prayer or humility, rather He was those things before them. He was such a demonstration of communion with the Father, that they begged Him to teach them how. The kneeling figure of their Master washing their feet was all the teaching on humility they needed.

So life Himself let them see how this life behaved under even the harshest of conditions. They listened, watched and were apprenticed. They rapidly discovered that they were totally unable to live this way. They were beholders of a life they could not produce. At His resurrection, He breathed that life into them, the life that man can never originate, only receive. They had already been apprenticed as to how it was to be lived out. Their initial apprenticeship over, they went into the world to teach others who had received the gift of life how He had taught them to live it out. They went to suffering men to minister the gifts of the Spirit, as they had watched Him, and as He had instructed: "The works that I do, shall you do also."

Christianity has utterly failed if it reduces that life summed in His person to a system of ethics or a way of virtuous living. To do so is to destroy it.

The Good News centered in Jesus Christ is that it is God's eternal purpose to have a vast family of sons who will ultimately be as much like the only Son, as it is possible for the finite to be like the infinite. Jesus accomplished that purpose by taking the race into His all-inclusive death and rising again, the head of a new race, a new family breathing His Spirit into all who believe.

Nor is the life of Jesus mocking the believers, for through His blood-shedding and resurrection, that life is given to us that He may become the first of many brothers and sisters. By the new birth, we are in union with Him. We do not become Him, but we discover our true selves in dying to self-love and surrendering to Him, becoming the willing expression of His life instead of our own. It is this that is the badge of the Christian before the world. He has a life that can only be finally explained in terms of the work of Jesus Christ, the Son of God. "By this all men will know that you are My disciples, if you have love one for another." Not because of church-going, or acceptance of a right creed or memorization of Scripture, however good those things may be. The world would know that we were apprenticed to that life, because they would be able to see in us the same love that had been first seen in Him. In a finite sense, the Word has become flesh in us.

Christianity is the life that is Jesus Christ now in us by the gift of His Spirit. That life must be demonstrated for all to see. If an opinion concerning ethics was all that we were talking about, then a textbook would do. But this life was

110

originally lived in an authentic human life; it can only be proclaimed in the context of its actual demonstration in a human life. Only God can *impart* that gift of life, on the basis of the shed blood of Christ and through His Spirit dynamically within us, but He has chosen that the *expression* of that life through our humanity shall be taught by those who have already learned to live it. Like the flu, it cannot be caught from the reading of a medical text, but rather from contact with someone who has the virus.

A newborn believer can hardly believe the Good News he has heard and now knows is true. The love of God freely toward him, the death of Christ that absolves him from all sin, so that there is now no condemnation, the promise of a life that is nothing short of Christ living within—this is all incredible, too good to dare to believe.

He is brought to the Body of Christ and received by a community of people who *are* this love in demonstration, the love of God reaching toward him. They love him and receive him with the love the Good News spoke of. God, he cannot touch, but these people he can. They tell him that his sins are forgiven through Christ and *then treat him as if he is.* In that company, he sees the life in actual demonstration. Looking at them, he can say, "So this is how I live out this Life given me by grace." The Bible is no longer remote, for what the older believers are demonstrating is explained in the Scripture. They could point to their lives and say, "this," and then to Scripture, "is that."

I slumped in my chair behind my desk in the church office. Old doubts flooded my mind making me wish I had never pursued these verses. What on earth was I thinking! Did I think I was Jesus Christ to call people to follow my example? What if I taught them error? I was not infallible in my understanding of truth. As for living the life, I was still learning and learning with many stumbles and mistakes.

His word rose in me. These doubts were the very areas that made discipling by imperfect men so important. In learning from an imperfect life the new converts would learn how to deal with their own failures to live out all that they knew. One of the first and ever present pitfalls of the Christian life is discouragement over failure, leading to despair. The greatest lesson a babe in Christ had to learn was how to receive forgiveness, get up and walk on rejoicing in Christ without condemnation.

It would be good for my little group to hear me honestly admit I did not know the answer to some of their questions and have them join me in the adventure of receiving light and understanding from God. My doubts rested in uneasy silence, still awed at this responsibility. I took comfort that Paul had said that the treasure he shared was contained in earthen vessels of a frail human life.

This explained to me one of the great puzzles of my study of the New Testament. I had long pondered the conversion of Saul of Tarsus and wrestled with a question I could not answer. The Christ-hating Pharisee on his way to Damascus to imprison all who called upon Jesus as Lord is confronted by the risen Christ. In that moment of light and miracle, Saul is born again. His immediate confession was that Jesus Christ was Lord and director of his life. "Lord, what will you have me to do?" was an expression of his yieldedness and faith.

I had no problem with that. He had met with Jesus, the ascended Lord, and had been born again without human help or persuasion. The question that had nagged me for years was, why could Jesus not have healed him and filled him with the Spirit as sovereignly as He had saved him? Why, at that point, bring in Ananias, an unknown disciple at Damascus, and have him introduce Paul to the first steps of the Christian life? It was Ananias who laid hands on Saul,

112

that he might be healed and filled with the Spirit. It was this simple believer of Damascus who probably took him to water and baptized him, and who introduced him to the believers in the city. *God, do you realize what you are doing? That man is going to write half the New Testament, and you have put him in the hands of Ananias to teach him the first principles of this life.* Why couldn't you who saved him, teach him, heal him and handle it alone? Why bring frail humans into this?

Now I saw why. The imparting of life is God's alone. We come into the Body of Christ by the regenerating action of the Holy Spirit alone. But as soon as we are in the Body, some Ananias must take us, lead us through an apprenticeship and teach us how to express the life so sovereignly given to us.

Jesus had said that the coming of the Holy Spirit was to be characterized by the recipients *being* witnesses, *not doing witnessing*. It is one thing to hand a new believer a tract on the victorious life; it is quite another to give yourself as a working if imperfect model of how to live it. Only as we give ourselves to *be* witnesses can we adequately proclaim God's word.

Ananias could have lectured Saul on the grace of God and given him tracts to read on justification by faith. Instead he said, *"Brother* Saul" and in that statement acknowledged that Saul's sin was gone and he was a member of God's family, accepted as a brother. His outstretched arms of greeting were a tangible extension of God's love embracing him.

Paul in turn did not write theological books, except maybe Romans. He and all the other writers of the New Testament present us with letters they wrote to each other, extensions of their human selves, full of laughter and tears. Through those lives, God's word comes to us exhorting and explaining the art of living this life in Christ.

I was convinced and completely sold on God's method of establishing His kingdom on earth. More than that, I was overwhelmed with the wonder of it; that we should be workers together with Him. I was also free from the bondage of having to set up a plan of discipling. The only plan, I knew now, was to be willing to give myself to those given to me by the King. It was a relief to know that there was no school of discipleship that followed a textbook. His school of discipleship conducts its lectures in strange places and with no formal announcement of class. All He needed was an individual Christian who was willing to live a normal, honest life before those He sent to learn the *how* of expressing Christ within.

Again I remembered Ray and those early vital days he had spent with Floyd and myself learning by watching to do what we were saying. If only I had those days over again to enthusiastically cooperate with what the Spirit was doing!

But there was the future, and already our numbers were swelling with young men hungry to know God and His word. To be in the school was a discipling for anyone who had ears and eyes, but in the sense of totally giving myself, I could not disciple everyone. But I could trust God to do the screening and selecting for me; He would put in my path those who were to become in a real way apprentices to what I had learned of Christ in living and ministry. At this time I did not have to look further than those who had been with us from the beginning, along with one or two latecomers.

I did not announce any of the deep dealings of God to anyone. I felt that to announce it would make people think that I was setting up a program and inviting adherents. As we flowed on in the Spirit, I had a feeling it would just *happen* so naturally we would hardly notice it. But ironically, the first observable effect was not among the students. It was in the auditorium meetings in New Jersey, where I became aware of a new flow of life and love.

The magnetism of the large crowds had been an issue with me ever since I had entered the ministry. In those early days I had equated large crowds with success. I had clung to the pulpit or lectern with white knuckles, thrilled at seeing the crowd being ministered to by the Spirit. And, the Spirit had ministered, in spite of my misplaced affection, and had gently brought me to that afternoon that showed me what loving people *really* means. In His light, I had relinquished anything the crowds might have given to me and surrendered to the expressing of His costly love for whomever He would send across my path. But a strange thing happened: in letting them go, I received them back free to love them for who they were, not what they did for me.

Death to any area of self only looks like death when we evaluate it from the self-grasping point of view. The fact is that Christ endured all the pain and actual death for us, leaving only the experience of resurrection for us. As we embrace death to the self-grasping principle, we find not death as we expected, but rather life.

I had always seen it as either the mass meetings or a handful, but now, on the other side of resurrection, I saw with clear vision: it was not an either/or situation. Jesus ministered to multitudes while giving Himself to the smaller group. Paul, too, ministered to multitudes while working more closely with the Timothys and smaller groups.

I found also that by opening up and giving myself to the few providentially placed in my path, a new release was given to love a crowd and from that day a new stream of life issued through the ministry.

XII

By now we had around twenty students in the school. We were well into the teaching of the major doctrines of the Scripture. The discipling took place inside that framework but was something quite distinct and apart. As it developed some of the young men, and Joanne among the girls, knew a clear calling to some kind of ministry that would demand a lifetime involvement. I witnessed the reality of this in most of the cases and began to apprentice them.

The apprenticing occurred spontaneously with no observable program or formal course. Wherever I happened to be ministering or counseling, some of them were with me, listening, watching and asking questions. In my study of the Gospels I had noted that Jesus rarely gave answers until questions were asked. When answers are given before questions have been thoroughly formed in our minds, we often do not recognize them as answers.

It was by closely observing a teacher of the Scripture that I had learned to teach. At the time I had not recognized it as discipleship, and certainly it was a far cry from what I now understood. The Bible school I had attended failed me in homiletics and quite rightly so. Looking over my final sermon, the teacher advised me to forget about preaching and concentrate on working as a deacon in a church.

After leaving Bible school I sensed a craving to communicate truth and felt the total inability to do so. My helplessness drove me to take the train or hitch a car ride into London from wherever I happened to be and join the crowds who walked, cycled or drove to Westminster Chapel each Friday night. The occasion was a Bible study and the speaker was the prince of Bible expositors, Dr. D. Martyn Lloyd-Jones. The building stood in its narrow street; the inside was bare and uninviting, the pews uncomfortably hard, but it did not stop the hundreds that regularly poured through its doors month after month to hear the Scripture expounded.

"The Doctor" as he was affectionately called, clothed in a Geneva gown surveyed the congregation over his glasses, his eyes bright and intense under the dome of his forehead. He opened the great pulpit Bible to the passage for the evening, and hundreds of pencils began to scratch out notes.

He and I never met on an informal basis, and he was not aware that in the vast crowd was a young man learning to teach by observing him. Week by week he expounded another verse of the Scripture. He took the text apart, showing what was there, how it all fit into the overall revelation of Scripture, and how it applied to life in the twentieth century.

But it was not to learn doctrine or to be fed spiritually that sent me to the chapel, but rather to see how he expounded Scripture. My notes were on *what* he was doing and *how* he was doing it. My first efforts showed I had no idea how he was doing it, but gradually I could anticipate him. At the

117

same time my own bumbling efforts at preaching each week in the church where I was trying to be a pastor began to communicate what was locked up inside me. I had a long way to go, but I had learned by listening.

In the same way the young men began to accompany me to the meetings in New Jersey. They sat with pen and notebook, not to listen to what I was saying, but to observe what I was doing in the presentation of truth with life. The ability to proclaim truth in the power of the Spirit is a sovereign gift of the Spirit. If God has not given it, no school or individual can put it there. But if it has been given, it must be developed and this is done better by a personal demonstration than by a textbook.

After the services we sat in a diner and talked. Ray always had outlined my teaching as he listened, carefully noting all I did, and where I was going. I gave him my own notes, and we discussed them together. As he became more observant, he told me where I had been weak in my argument. I rejoiced to see how he was becoming able to help me.

Questions flowed freely. Why did I follow that theme from the text? How did I know that was the message for tonight? How did I know when to stop? They had felt we could have gone on all night. Why did we sing that particular Scripture before I spoke? Was it a random idea, did we like the tune, or was it because the Spirit told us? If so, how do you know the voice of the Spirit?

We sat late over coffee discussing the need to recognize the voice of God within us, and to depend on Him. We discussed also the need for human preparation. Ministering is not only the outlining of truth in a way that it can be communicated, it must begin with a revelation of truth by the Spirit and in its preparation and delivery there must be constant dependence on the Spirit. If human preparation is not there, then words are empty air, but if the Spirit is not

118

there, there is no ministry. This dependence on the Spirit can never be taught in a textbook, but it can be recognized and described in an on-the-job apprenticeship.

But public preaching is a very small part of ministering. The man who only preaches will be answering questions no one is asking. Any of these young men who would stand before multitudes one day, had to learn that only in dealing with individuals, loving one or two, and leading them from darkness to light, could their public ministry be with power and love.

Very soon I knew that most of these who were with me would one day have a flock of their own to lead through a maze of problems. They would have their own spiritual babes and face up to the fact that Christianity offers a radical and continual change of life.

The radical change is not something that just happens mysteriously. As Joanne had discovered, faith, even if it is not this world's logic, is not illogical, but based on the firm foundation of what Christ did in His death and triumphant resurrection.

Some who had come from evangelical backgrounds had used the Bible almost as a book of magic phrases; "the Bible says" prefaced a panacea for whatever problem was to be faced. Or they had been taught to lay hands on the problem and pray. That is all well and good, but it is no use telling a person that they mustn't worry, or they should cheer up and praise God, or they should stop doing this or that sinful habit. The work that Jesus did on the cross has got to probe deeply into their problem, and be practically applied. The Bible is not a holy spell-book full of phrases to be hurled at people. It rather is a description of the life that flows out of the resurrection and outpoured Spirit.

To many of them this was the most thrilling aspect of these days together. The fact that Jesus Christ is now Lord on earth in the Holy Spirit means that every problem in man can be solved. No one is hopeless who will surrender to Jesus Christ the Lord. One of the students described this as having his mind baptized with hope. He could face the most hopeless cases radiating hope that they would change because he now could see that the Spirit, coming through the word of God changed us, if we were willing to be changed. This ability to see through the situation to what God sees, and to be willing to speak, and to expect with hope is the beginning of true ministry.

Others found the beginning of hope came with a new understanding of faith. They had failed to keep their promises to God so many times, that any hope of a change in their lives was in an elusive final dedication that they never made. Now they saw the shift from *their* promises to God, to *His* final promise in the finished work of Christ to them.

The old man has gone, not because the Christian had finally made an adequate dedication to God, but because Jesus has adequately taken the old us to death in His death. The new man, the believer, *is,* not because he feels that he is new, but because Jesus rose again and carried him into the Spirit. Because he is new, and the old has gone, he can now put off the old ways, and put on the new life of Christ, his true new self.

Some of the young men came with me on a retreat in a cabin nestled on the side of the Catskill Mountains. After praying and waiting on God for most of the morning we discussed these things over a light lunch. The boys did not grasp what I was trying to say, and the subject was dropped.

We decided to go for a walk. An abandoned cart track, its ruts overgrown with grass wound its way through the woods that blazed in autumn foliage. Reds, browns and yellows surrounded us, all bathed in the pools of the warm fall sun that poured through the open branches above us. I pointed to the leaves that hung brown and yellowed on the trees. "When do those leaves die?" I questioned. "Will they be dead when they fall off or do they fall off because they are dead?"

One of the boys lit up "I've got it! They fall off because they *are* dead. They died when the sap stopped flowing to them. We are dead to the self principle when we rest in His work for us, and because we are dead we can put away all the old life style and put on the new self—the new sap—the life of Jesus."

So many people despair because areas of their lives are not what they will be, but when our eyes are on what He has already accomplished we can rest—assured that He who began the work will complete it.

With that kind of hope we can drag sin into the light calling it by name and deal with it. It *can* go, and shall be replaced by the expression of Christ. To see that is to have hope. The Christian looks at himself with hope expecting the old ways to go, and actively cooperating with the Spirit.

While in Puerto Rico, I had watched a lizard shed its skin. It inched out of it finally and walked away with a beautiful new skin. I realized that the only reason the lizard could get rid of his skin was that *he already had a new one underneath.* That's why the old one itched and couldn't be lived with.

So the Christian is a new person, Christ within him is his life, and the way he used to be itches. It has to go so that the Christ life, his real new self, may be seen. It is mockery to tell a person who is not yet born again to change. They cannot, for they have nothing to replace what they are.

The Christian can be confronted with truth. He can be helped to peel off the old skin and be who he really is— Christ in him. We must be involved in that change. Only God can regenerate us, *but we work out our salvation.* The Bible assumes that we are going to change, and it assumes we are going to have a part to play in that change, so it addresses its commands to us, to act on the basis and in the light of what Christ has done.

For instance, as we had learned in the early days, there is a biblical way to forgive others, even as there is a biblical way to handle sorrow, suffering, temptation, anger, self-pity, depression, and guilt. The church has left all this to psychiatrists over the last fifteen or twenty years, but all of the shucking off of these sinful life styles can only be done by an application of what Jesus accomplished on the cross, in the power of the Spirit.

The truth is, we often don't feel like living consistently with who we are in Christ. And the New Testament understands perfectly well that our feelings will not always agree. Why else would it command us to live out the person we now are in Christ? We have lived out of our feelings as a source of action in the world, we have now come to the kingdom of light, where Jesus is King. *The kingdom of God is not a democracy* but a *love dictatorship.* The One who commands us is the one who died for us.

It is a new way. Whether we *feel* like forgiving, or giving our anger up to God is not the issue. We as subjects of the kingdom of Jesus respond to His word, and expect the power of the Spirit. Because of this, the Christian's hope is for rapid movement away from the old way to the expressing of Christ. He really can do all things through Christ who strengthens him. People who have struggled all their lives can expect a rapid change when the triumph of Christ is applied specifically to their problem.

The fellows and girls learned this, and also saw that as in public ministry, so with the individual we depend on the Spirit to give the word out of our understanding of the resurrection that uniquely fits the problem that we presently face. The biggest danger was to go spiritually high and throw out life-changing prescriptions with a holier-than-thou attitude. They had to learn patience and meekness in applying the Good News in Christ.

Part of that was in having it work in their own lives. In restaurants, walking in forests, or around a table in the church kitchen we sat and shared these principles, applying them to our lives, sharing our struggles and problems. The first thrill matured to a steady confident hope.

I looked at them one day eagerly discussing someone who had recently come to Christ and how best he could be helped. I looked at Ray and Louis. They were no longer hippies, or ex-hippies. They were Christ's ministry gifts to the church in the making, and much of the making was already over. I remembered the phone call when I had been asked to let the "ex-hippies" testify and my reply had been that they needed to be apprenticed. They were now well into that apprenticeship, and down within me I knew that they were ready to make some mistakes with supervision. But I cringed at the idea. Counsel, direct, preach—"but they are dealing with *lives,* and if they say something wrong . . ." I pleaded with myself. "That's where *your* supervision comes in. You correct their mistakes, and they can put everything right, and learn without hurting anyone," said a voice within me.

Mistakes had to be. Struggle was a necessity. I vividly remembered watching a butterfly emerge from a chrysalis. It struggled for nearly a day before it emerged in all its beauty and flew away. I contemplated another one in the early stage of struggle, and decided to help it, by delicately splitting open its prison with a razor blade. The beautiful creature was free without a struggle, but it died very soon for it had no muscle to fly with. In the wonder of God's creation, the wing muscles are strengthened in the struggle to get out of the chrysalis. These disciples had to be shown how, but then they had to get out there and *do,* and in their mistakes and failures their spiritual muscles would develop in the struggles of experience, and they would become mature believers able to lead others out of their own experience. The mistakes would be good, for with supervision, each mistake would lead to the right way of doing it.

Around this time I read Romans 15:4. The word that stood out for me was "able to *admonish* one another." The word "admonish" was what we were talking about. It means to confront another with truth, with a view to helping them to change for their good. Paul said that these people were now able thus to bring powerful help—their qualifications he lists as filled with goodness—that warm concern that gives me interest in another's growth and filled with knowledge of the truth. They now had a working knowledge of truth, as well as concern—and this Scripture said they were able.

Ray began to get invitations to preach, and we did not stop him. He was *able to admonish* in public and private. The tapes of his messages came back to me and I listened with joy. His messages had all the faults of a young preacher and the big fault that he sounded like me, but the main thing was that he flowed in life and was saying what God was saying. As bookings came to me that I could not take, I suggested they contact Ray. Many times I closed my eyes as I said it, afraid that he would say the wrong thing, but only enthusiastic reports came back. And now I almost wanted to hold him back, so I could enjoy having him as a disciple. I had missed so much with him, because I had fought the whole idea. Now I wanted to have him with me, but I knew he was on his way to being himself a fisher of men.

When students came to Matawan in New Jersey, they joined me on the platform to teach Scripture songs. I began to urge the people to talk to them and share their problems. I had the same desire to close my ears, in case I should hear them make a mistake, but in the diner afterward, as they told me what they had said, I realized they had given the correct answers, had heard the Spirit and spoken what He had given them to say. They *were* able to admonish.

At one of the Matawan meetings, a young man approached me and begged me to find time in my schedule to visit their prayer group. I was sorry, there was no way that I could fit it in. Then I hesitated, "There is a young man, Ray Ciervo. He's just over there talking to someone, the fellow with the black hair. Why don't you ask him?" Out of that Ray began a regular Saturday-night Bible study in a large home in mid-Jersey. He began to take with him some other students to help and to watch. He was beginning to have his own disciples.

As Floyd and I talked over how we could best help these young men emerging from their chrysalises of learning, in a practical way, we recognized that within a short time we knew Ray and the others would be shepherds of their own flocks. In my own Bible training, the practical experience I had received was almost nil. I had two regular duties. One was to go and knock on doors trying to make people listen to the Gospel, when they wanted to be watching television. The other was going to a senior citizens' home to preach and sing to the very old and very senile. Both of these exercises were not the best preparation for what was ahead.

I was never taught how to conduct holy communion in the power of the Spirit, or how to bury the dead in the triumph of resurrection or how to baptize a new believer. Small matters—until it has to be done. I still remember the stark terror the first time I waded into the water to baptize a new convert. It was a minor miracle I didn't drown both of us! Both Floyd and I decided that these were the areas in which the boys needed practical training. The next time I baptized, Ray came into the water with me.

It was a thrilling moment as I stood in the water with Ray opposite me and a new believer between us. We held the young man and prayed that he would receive the Holy Spirit, and walk in the power of the resurrection. I then said, "Upon the confession of your faith I baptize you in the name of the Father, and of the Son, and of the Holy Spirit. Amen." and then plunged him into the water, burying his past in this act of faith in the work Christ accomplished. We brought him out of the water and helped him up the steps into the towel held by one of the brothers. As I guided him into the towel, I suddenly relived three years previously when I had been guiding Ray up those same steps and the Spirit had forcibly said, "He's in your hands." A lump rose in my throat and I wanted to weep, laugh and praise God. A hippie, saved, Spirit-filled and apprenticed to the exercising of his ministry, able to admonish, now standing with me in the water baptizing another.

I raised my hands in praise to God, and led the congregation in singing *Amazing Grace*.

That summer of 1974 we took most of the students to a week-long camp where I was speaking. It gave us precious hours together, and opportunity for them to minister after the meetings. They stayed on the campground but often came to visit the farm where I was staying just outside the town.

It was a beautiful antique farm, owned by Wayne and Yvonne Miller who delighted to open everything up to these fellows and girls from Brooklyn. They gave us lunch in the orchard one day. I waited for it sprawled under a tree. Beside me were two or three of the boys who had been sharing and questioning concerning the true nature of

126

humility. Now we had stopped and lay drinking in the scene. Mennonite ladies, their white head-coverings bobbing as they came with their covered dishes and desserts, were busy at the tables. Through the leaves of the trees above us I watched through half-closed eyes the white clouds drift lazily across the sky.

Someone broke the silence. "We have played in the barn, herded hogs, and then sat here and rapped about humility—and I have seen it today, I mean *I understand humility*. You know, I'm on fire with it inside." He sat up and stared across the fields, "When are we closest to Jesus' way of doing things, sitting under a tree rapping about humility, or sitting on a pew listening to a lecture?"

No answer was needed for we all knew. I knew because I had seen that *being with* is the only way to finally teach. They knew because they had learned well. They called us for lunch and we scrambled to our feet.

"But always remember," I cautioned, "Jesus habitually went to the synagogue every Sabbath and worshiped with the covenant community. If we are not in vital fellowship with the covenant community we are all finished."

XIII

For a long weary year Joanne had been in a dark tunnel of failure and doubt. In it she had proven conclusively that the grace of God worked, and she had emerged with a proven understanding of His salvation. With Christ living His life within her she had found total answers to her specific problems. She knew God personally now, on a firsthand basis, with the solid platform of Christ's work for her as the foundation of her faith.

Out of her experience developed a sense of responsibility to share this faith with everyone. And so she ended up going with Ray and the group that traveled with him on a Saturday night. In the large room where Ray held his meeting Jo sat and listened to how he presented truth. Afterward coffee was served, and in her enthusiasm to share with anyone who had a problem she appeared almost rude. Her eagerness to listen brought her face to face with problems she could not answer.

Here, for instance, were Christians who could not forgive, who walked in endless circles of bitterness and grudges over the past. She didn't know how to apply what Christ had done to such situations, but she was confident that there *was* an answer. She was aflame with hope. "I don't know the answer, but I'll pray and get it," she told them frankly. "When I do, I'll share it with you."

The next time we were all together, she shared the problem, and we had a spontaneous study on forgiveness. In this way she would listen to problems, and gradually learn to apply God's answer.

It was as if she had come to know God personally, and was now discovering practically, in a maze of different situations, that here was final truth that always worked. Jeremiah 9:24 in her Amplified Bible put together how she felt. "But let him who glories glory in this, that he understands and knows Me (Personally and practically, directly discerning and recognizing My Character), that I am the Lord Who practices loving-kindness, judgment and righteousness in the earth; for in these things I delight, says the Lord."

One night she thought about what was going on. These people were so much like herself. Having been sovereignly awakened and reborn, long months of struggle followed before she finally gulped in the fresh air of God's grace with understanding. She was reading John 11, and verse 44 leaped out at her. "He who had died came forth, bound hand and foot with wrappings; and his face was wrapped around with a cloth. Jesus said to them, 'Unbind him, and let him go.' "

She turned the words over and over. "Unbind him, and let him go." Lazarus had been raised from the dead by a miracle, but he was still encased in grave clothes. He was alive but encased in the wrappings of death. It was not another miracle that freed him. Those standing by were commanded to unbind him so that he would be free to live the life that had been given to him.

That had been her experience. She had been life encased, struggling to be free, born of the light, yet still living in the darkness of legalism. It had been the teaching of God's grace from us that had loosed her and allowed her freely to enjoy salvation.

"It was the *renewal* of my mind to think God's thoughts that allowed me to understand and see what He had done and was doing." She chuckled as she thought of the old way of handling the Christian life, which was to seek peace by the *removal* of the mind!

In reading John 11, she knew God had spoken a ministry to her. I realized it, too, as she shared it with me. She radiated a vibrant intensity as she outlined what the Spirit had said to her.

I had begun meetings in Wayne, New Jersey, and she was able to come to the second meeting. The auditorium was a cold barn of a gymnasium that was not suitable for any kind of public speaking. Our voices echoed and bounced through the vastness in temperatures that were never really warm. I could see Jo in the audience. Her eyes were alight, and she was hardly able to wait to confront her Lazarus, to unbind and let go. This is how she later described the last part of the meeting:

"Then Malcolm called for the sick, those needing salvation, Baptism in the Holy Spirit, and so on, to slip out of their seats and meet us at the back for counseling. I had prayed, as I scanned the assembly, that God would send one person to *me*, and that I would not have to seek anyone out.

"One girl slipped out of her seat, and I practically ran up the aisle to meet her. I've finally got a live one, I thought. I soberly escorted her to the special counseling room. She was wringing her hands and was only too glad to pour out her problem. It seemed that she had a recurring case of athlete's foot. . . .

130

"As ridiculous as it seemed, I began to pray for this earnest young girl, only I could have chosen my words in prayer a little better. I blurted out, 'Father, you are in this girl from the top of her head to the bottom of her feet.' As I realized what I had said, I began to laugh. This sort of put this girl off (the very *idea* of *laughing* at such a time). And I oddly wondered if Kathryn Kuhlman had gotten her start this way. . . .

"I was tempted to ask the same thing of God that the Israelites asked: 'Lord, before us is the Red Sea. Are you sure you haven't made a mistake just this once?' But I knew all too well that God's way is perfect, and *I* am in His way. Glory to God.

"Afterward, Malcolm asked me how it went. When I shared my 'counselee's' problem, he responded in his usual shepherdly concern and support—he cracked up. . . ."

This amusing and humbling beginning was in no way typical of what happened in the weeks that followed. God had undoubtedly given Joanne a ministry of peeling off grave clothes, and she developed a Spirit-given discernment for getting to the root of people's problems, and helping them deal with them in the power of the Spirit. She had arranged her work schedule so that she could take off most of the summer and travel with my wife, Jean, and me in meetings. Throughout the summer we traveled as a family, and there proved to be many times when we would mutually benefit by her being along. And Bobby and one or two others planned to be with us in some of the camps, too.

The first camp of the summer was a Mennonite retreat center in Pennsylvania called Mt. Zion. It was a family camp, and I had invited one of our students to conduct children's services during the adult meetings. But as we were packing our last suitcase we suddenly discovered that she would be unable to come.

131

I shuddered at the prospect of what the week would be like. Normally parents tried to leave their children home when they came to a Bible study, but the advertising had specifically assured everyone that there would be charismatic meetings for children. I could imagine the place overrun with children who would normally be left home, all eagerly awaiting their own evangelist, only to find we had none. Disgruntled and bored, they would sit, crawl, fall and cry in the evening Bible study. I gave an involuntary shudder: children coming out of the woodwork and no hope of getting an evangelist for them at this late date.

I half-heartedly praised God for the situation as we drove out to the restaurant where we had arranged to meet Joanne, Bobby and the other students who had been able to find their way clear to come. We sat, outlining what the week held for each one, and what I expected of them. Jo and Bobby were to head up whatever happened after the service and were to be ready for counseling throughout the day. Then I looked at Jo, and said hesitatingly, "Jo, how would you like to be a charismatic child evangelist for about a week?"

"What?" she croaked, her eyes widening in mock horror. "Me? Oh, no. I just don't have it with kids! I'm kind of a little old lady around them. They get on my nerves when they make noise—" She faltered, and fell silent. "I guess I can sing and play to them," she finally said.

I nodded, "You know, if you're ever going to speak to adults, it will certainly help to have experience with children. That's how I began." It was true what I was saying but I became aware that I was trying to sell her on it, and so I said no more. That was up to the Holy Spirit. She would have to pray her way through this, solo. At length her smile came of its own bidding, and she shrugged, "I'll do what I can and trust the Lord."

It was the first morning of camp, and those of us from the school sat together rather sleepily at the breakfast table. I threw out the question to all of them, "Have you ever led anyone into the Baptism in the Holy Spirit?" Jo half shrugged, implying she might have had something to do with it and Bobby said that he had prayed with some. No one seemed to be sure.

I knew exactly what they meant, for this was how I had responded for the first four years of my ministry as a Pentecostal pastor. Although I had received all the teaching regarding the necessity for the Spirit-filled life, no one told me how to actually lead someone to receive. It was like having a lecture on hammer and nails with no one giving a clue as to how to nail together two pieces of wood.

In the early days of my ministry I groped for a way to bring my congregations to be baptized in the Spirit. I pastored Christians in East Anglia, a section of England that had been cut off from the main flow of English life for centuries. It was an area filled with farms set in the middle of fields either sown with crops or used as grazing land for cattle. Hamlets of thatched-roofed cottages clustered around the market square and the village church.

I preached among these happy, simple farming folk, and they came seeking to be filled with the Holy Spirit. I laid my hands on them and prayed loudly and long. Nothing happened. But then, no one expected anything to happen—at least until one had "tarried" long enough, and as no one really knew how long that would take, no one questioned the endless laying on of hands.

Our ministry moved to Northern Ireland. The windswept mountains of Mourne and the wild desolate beaches of Donegal became my prayer closet where I walked alone for hours seeking how to bring people to *experience* God. I was appointed to be a youth evangelist in the Pentecostal churches. Parents had been born again and Spirit-filled years before, and now their children coasted on their parents' experiences of God. They were bored with their second-hand religion, and I began to direct my message at the necessity of a personal experience of the Holy Spirit. Afterward many would come and ask me to pray for them. I thankfully sent them to their pastor who, as a Pentecostal pastor, surely knew how to pray for them. Often, unfortunately, this wasn't the case, and after all the noise was over, the disillusioned seeker went home. The experience had eluded him.

Some of these began to contact me and ask me to have meetings where they could *get* what I was talking about. I stalled, because I knew I wasn't sure how they got what I was saying they had to have. In fact, I was also aware that many Pentecostals didn't know how they got what they had, and therefore didn't know whether they still had it most of the time.

I finally found a couple of older ministers, and another young fellow of my own age, Jim Kay, and booked a hotel for an Easter retreat. I decided I would preach on the Baptism in the Spirit, and the older men would pray with the seekers. We sent out the advertising, and immediately had a response that filled the hotel, as well as the one adjoining it. At some late date, the senior men got wind that I was leaving them to pray these seekers into Spirit-fullness. The day before we were to begin, I received a note from them apologizing that they would not be able to attend the retreat.

Two hotels full of people were looking to me to help them receive the Spirit, and the men I leaned on had now bowed out! I was scared to the point of weakness, and I wished I could silently slip out of town. I sank to my knees in my hotel room and cried out to God. All that preaching I had done for the last months! Now I had to practice what I preached, or forget about this forever.

It was 9 P.M. I had twelve hours before the retreat began, twelve hours to have God show me how to bring someone to the fullness of the Spirit. I prayed, I read and waited upon God Who only can give light. Principles began to dawn in my own soul, as I stood at the window of the hotel looking out over the moonlit waves of the Irish sea. Somewhere in the distance a clock struck twice. I was exhausted yet fired to go on. As the weekend began the following morning, desperate faith demanded I apply the principles I had learned the night before. And they worked! By Sunday evening everyone there had received the Spirit! I was elated. From then on, I could face seekers with more than just a kind of vague hopefulness.

I looked now at the rather confused faces sitting around the breakfast table and knew that they were confused for the same reason as I had been. They had prayed for believers to receive the Spirit. Possibly some actually had, in which case they had been as surprised as the seekers! But that kind of vague expectancy does not give any *hope* to the seekers. Over our eggs and bacon I shared what I knew.

One great misconception is that the Baptism in the Spirit is an initial receiving of the Spirit. The Spirit is initially received when we are born again, and if we do not have the Spirit in this sense, we do not belong to Him. To name Jesus as Lord of life is to say that the Spirit is within us working out that Lordship in a practical way. He within us is Christ within us, expressed in what Galatians 5:22 calls "the fruit *of the Spirit.*"

Jesus spoke of this to the disciples in the upper room. They were old-covenant Israelites, and Jesus said of them that the Holy Spirit was *with* them. He then referred to the day of His resurrection, as the day when the Spirit would no

135

longer be with them but actually *in* them. On that night of His resurrection, He breathed into them and said, "Receive the Holy Spirit" (John 20:22). A better translation of the original language would be, *"Receive here and now."*

In that moment they received all that we understand today as the new birth. All that Jesus died to give us is wrapped up in the Holy Spirit; He is the promise of all the Father gives us in Christ, and in the Spirit is all the Father gives us. He *is* the gift. In that moment, they entered the long promised kingdom of the Messiah and began to walk in the realm of the Spirit. This was their rebirth.

Similarly, we cannot know the fullness of the Spirit, until we have been born into the kingdom. "So find out first if the person seeking the Baptism in the Spirit is born again," I told them. "A lot of people assume that because they are in a church, or a member of the priesthood, a minister or Sunday school teacher, that they must be born again, and that's just not the case. Never take that for granted."

"Then, what *is* the Baptism in the Spirit?" one of the fellows asked, clearly frustrated. "In my church they always asked if a person 'had the Holy Ghost,' when they talked of the Baptism. What you are saying is that we have the Holy Ghost from our new birth on."

I reminded them of the Bible passages that described the Baptism in the Spirit as being a further knowledge and experiencing of this same Spirit. To those men into whom He had breathed the Spirit, He said that they would be *endued or clothed* with power from on high (Luke 24:49), that they would be *baptized* in the Spirit, or *immersed into* the Spirit (Acts 1:5). He described it as the Spirit who was in them coming *upon* them (Acts 1:8) and when it actually happened, it said they were all *filled* with the Spirit.

This happened on the day of Pentecost as a definite and final experience. He who already was their source and spring of life within now came upon their whole person, clothing them and gently directing them, as long as they let Him.

Peter laid down the norm for the Christian life in Acts 2:38. "And Peter said to them, 'Repent, and let each of you be baptized in the name of Jesus Christ for the forgiveness of your sins; and you shall receive the gift of the Holy Spirit.' "

Repentance that ends in baptism in water is the new birth, the faith that rests in Jesus, which cannot happen without the Spirit coming into us. But Peter states that *beyond* that was the receiving of the gift of the Spirit. This is the beginning of the Christian life as it is understood in the New Testament.

If this enduement with power is the promise of the Father, brought to us through what Jesus did, then we receive Him by faith, even as we received our salvation. We are not filled with the Spirit because we earned the right to such a blessing. We receive through what Christ has accomplished. We do not have to make promises and dedications in order to guarantee our mature use of the power, we rather rest in His promise to us. In that confidence we ask the Father for the gift of the Spirit.

Only when we see clearly that Jesus is the guarantee of our receiving the Spirit is it time to ask in strong confidence for the Baptism. "You are going to find a lot of confused people at this point," I warned the would-be counselors. "People think they will receive because they have been good church members, or because they have fasted or prayed half a night. Others think they will receive if one particular person prays for them. But this isn't so. You must lead them to see that God has guaranteed to fill them with His Spirit on the basis of what Christ has done for them."

This makes asking for the Baptism very simple. We do

not have to shout, or repeat words very quickly, trying to work ourselves up. We simply ask for Father's promise on the basis of what He has done for us.

Tongues are the big problem to many people. A person who is afraid of speaking in tongues is usually not ready to receive the Spirit—they are saying that God can come, but it must be on their terms. Anyone filled with the Spirit will speak in tongues, sooner or later.

Most people have problems because they are afraid that God will take their mouths out of control, pour languages through their vocal chords and make them look foolish. But this is not how God operates. *He never takes away our wills, or puts us beyond our choices.*

The miracle of tongues is in the giving of an utterance to the speech centers of our brain. This utterance we have never learned and do not understand, but it nevertheless fully expresses the mood of our spirit. When we are filled with the Spirit, we are aware of another language, or words inside us—and *we* must be willing to speak it out. Far from making us robots or puppets, the Baptism in the Spirit makes us full, authentic human beings.

I told them, "Ask any seeker these questions: 'Are you born again,' and ask them to share their testimony. 'Are you willing to ask the Father for the Spirit on the basis of what Christ has done?' having explained the foundation for such a hope, and 'Are you willing to speak in tongues when the Spirit gives the utterance?' Having explained all that, and when you discern that they are ready, begin to worship. Exalt the Lord Jesus who is the center of it all and *have them ask the Father* for the gift. You can lay hands on them if it seems right and you feel it would help," I said. "But for heaven's sake, move in the Spirit! Don't clap your hands on their head and press them and vibrate your hands 'with the power of the Spirit!' "

We were into our fourth cup of coffee by the time I had finished sharing this foundation for hope in leading someone to the fullness of the Spirit. It seemed to have cleared up a lot of problems, and Joanne looked very excited. "I prayed with someone the other day, who said that they thought they were making the tongues up. What do you say to them?"

"I usually read Luke 11:11-13 to them," I explained. "It is as if Jesus assured us that when we ask, we shall undoubtedly get what we ask for and not a counterfeit. 'Now suppose one of you fathers is asked by his son for a fish; he will not give him a snake instead of a fish, will he? Or if he is asked for an egg, he will not give him a scorpion, will he? If you then, being evil, know how to give good gifts to your children, how much more shall your Heavenly Father give the Holy Spirit to those who ask Him?' "

The kitchen girls had to come and clear dishes, so we left the dining area. I encouraged my group to make the teaching their own and to let the Spirit turn it into reality.

From all over north central Pennsylvania the crowds poured into the tent meeting. It was held on the grounds of Mt. Zion retreat house in the hamlet of Roaring Branch. The early arrivals stood in knots talking farm business and the latest they had seen God do in their home prayer meetings. Ruddy-faced men, feeling the awkwardness of their pressed suits greeted me as I walked from the house.

The place where the meetings were to be held was not exactly a tent, but a roof with no walls. Chairs and rough benches were placed in front of a platform where a song leader, who made up in enthusiasm what he lacked in musical knowledge, led everyone in singing with the help of an out-of-tune piano. The chairs and benches were soon filled with the mountain farmers heartily singing old hymns.

From where I sat on the platform I could see across the valley to the pine-covered hills on the other side. The sun finally sank in a blaze of golden glory behind the pines, bringing the valley into deep shadow. The lights were switched on and night insects of every description danced around them causing great moving shadows on the congregation. A chill breeze came up the valley surrounding us, and I brought my message to a close.

Joanne had been in another building holding her first children's meeting. She reappeared just as I was inviting those who wished to be born again, or Spirit-filled to come to the front where students could pray with them.

I motioned to Bobby and Joanne. "Please take all those seeking the Baptism outside; they are yours tonight." I quickly turned away from the pleading look of helplessness in Jo's eyes.

An hour later, I found them walking to the main kitchen. In an awed voice, Jo said, "They all received." She just shook her head in wonderment.

The next morning she sat down at breakfast and looked me right in the eye. "Let's not talk about the success with the Baptism in the Spirit," she said. "I need help with the children. They are a challenge like I never dreamed. How do I prepare a message?"

I asked her what she planned to speak on that night. Blinking at me through her glasses she said, "Working out our salvation." I caught my breath and asked if that wasn't rather heavy for children. It was, in fact, my text for that night meeting.

"No, I don't really think so," she said, tracing the rim of her cup with a finger. "These children testified and worshiped last night, and they want to know something more than Bible stories unrelated to life." I shifted uneasily; I had not expected her to do this. I wondered what the Mennonites that packed the tent would think.

I soon found out! The children went home and told their parents what they were receiving, and began to live it out on their own child-like level. The parents were deeply impressed and asked me how I trained her. "Oh—over a fried egg the other morning!"

Each day we talked about what she was doing, and each night she gained experience in child evangelism. During the day she counseled with Bobby and discovered with him a definite ministry of leading new converts into the Baptism in the Spirit.

As we drove out of Mt. Zion, I was awed at the way we three had worked together as a team, even though Jo and Bobby were still in the process of being apprenticed. By the end of the summer Joanne had a very clearly defined and established ministry of her own, yet she was still under my supervision. She had kept in touch with all the children that cared to write to her, a personal correspondence with nearly a hundred young people, not to mention other adults that she was able to help by mail. Another disciple was gradually moving out by herself.

XIV

Whenever God involves us deeply in a new work, it is usually as much for our own benefit, as anyone else's. The discipling of others accomplished something in my own life that was long overdue. The last months had been like the sun rising, shedding light in all directions, but this question clung like early morning mist. *What authority did I have to mold the lives of these fellows and girls?*

It was not enough to say that God had sent me. I had seen too many self-appointed religious dictators set up their little empires claiming God's authority. Nor was it enough to be able to prove my message was in the Scripture. That was of vital importance of course, but there had to be more than that. I was fallible and could be interpreting the Scriptures incorrectly. What were my credentials to be presented to would-be disciples?

I turned the question over and over in my mind. What is that invisible mantle called authority that clothed some and not others? When it was present, I had noted that it did not have to be proved, talked about or grasped after, for everyone, even its enemies, were aware of it. I also knew a number who spoke from Scripture and undoubtedly had an experience of the Spirit, but who lacked authority. To make up for the lack, they grasped at any straw in the wind that might give the impression that they did indeed have authority. A man will make much of a title or an academic degree, insist on a special seat at important gatherings and services, wear distinctive dress, and make demands that he be obeyed. All of this does not add up to authority.

Authority is not something we take to ourselves, but rather something we receive from God. Too many times we have rushed into some project assuming that God will automatically give us authority to carry out every idea we have. Only when we are a spokesman for Him, doing what His present purpose for us is, can we expect His authority to be present. When God sends us with His word, He always anoints us with the Spirit of power to do what He sent us to do. He also provides authority that somehow makes people hear. I had gradually learned that there were many areas in which I had lacked power and had wound up groping for authority—because I had *not* been sent.

Authority, then, is bestowed by God, on the one submitted to Him. It enables us to do what He has ordered us to do. Only as we are submitted to God do we have authority with men. When it is present in a man his presentation of truth is credible. He is marked out as an ambassador of Jesus the Lord and safe to be imitated.

But to say that we are submitted to God is too vague. What did that mean practically worked out? Where and what is God's channel for His authority on earth? In Matthew 28:18, Jesus announced His universal authority: "All authority has been given to Me in heaven and on earth." He then addressed the disciples, that in the light of that they were to go about their work of teaching with authority. "Go therefore and make disciples. . . ." In His Ascension, He is crowned with universal authority, and He invests that in His Church on earth.

When we say that, we must be very careful to understand that the Church, the kingdom of God, is made up of those who are reborn. In fact, *unless* we are born again, we do not see the Church, nor can enter into it (John 3).

It is through the company of the reborn in any locality that Christ expresses His authority on earth. This community is therefore called the Body of Christ, which is to Christ what my body is to me. "Body of Christ" is more than an illustration of this relationship, it is rather an exact parallel. Every member of my body has a relationship to the head and is submitted to it for action and direction. But also, each member is as vitally related to the rest of the body and is submitted to all the other members. In this way, no member of my body acts in accord with the will of the head without acting in harmony with every other member at the same time.

The word "submit" translates the Greek word meaning "to stand under," "to be arranged in orderly fashion." There is no order to the body without submission, and there is no order or authority in the Body of Christ without it. The New Testament communities of believers saw themselves "standing under" Christ and because of that, standing under each other, ready to learn and receive. Paul wrote Ephesians 5:21, "And be subject to one another in the fear of Christ." And it was the thought behind Philippians 2:3, "Do nothing from selfishness or empty conceit, but with humility of mind, let each of you regard one another as more important than himself." We cannot function without each other, for the power of God is not invested in one individual but in the company together, the Body which,

144

functioning in harmony, is the expression of Christ on earth.

One individual cannot fully express Christ, *except* in concert with the others. When one individual publicly expresses Christ, he does so only because of the many unseen members that have contributed to the work.

This had always been a blank spot in my life. I saw the Church as the company of the born-again, but I never did see that I needed anyone to help me accomplish the will of God. It seemed eons ago that I had thought of Christianity as a spectator sport, where the many sat in congregations watching the chosen few accomplish great things for God. Much had changed since then, and my understanding of fellowship had brought a clear understanding of our need for each other. Now I thrilled to its far-reaching implications, as I searched for the meaning of authority.

My authority was that I was doing what God had called me to, in harmony with the teaching of Scripture, as I was living in submission to the local expression of the Body of Christ. My message and direction were not only received from God but also echoed and witnessed to by the other elders of the Body.

I saw this supremely in Jesus. It is said of Him in the Bible that He spoke as one that had authority and not as the other religious leaders. Jesus perfectly walked our human road, and in His authority as the perfect human, He had the authority out of His submission to His Father. The first recorded incident of His life after babyhood was the visit to the temple at the age of twelve. It was an important event in the life of a Jewish boy, when he was examined on his understanding of the Law that he had been taught since his first glimmer of understanding. For the first twelve years of his life he was taught at home and by the local rabbi. Then came the trip to Jerusalem, for *bar mitzvah,* when he became a son of the Law and responsible to God for his own spiritual life. After that he was counted as a man, and upon his return home began apprenticeship to his father's trade. This was emphasized by the fact he would go up to Jerusalem in the women's caravan but return with the men in a separate caravan.

This also explains why Mary and Joseph could miss Him for a day. Mary naturally thought He was with Joseph in the men's caravan, and Joseph assumed that He was too shy to join the men, so soon after *bar mitzvah.* When they found Him in the temple, Jesus' words are significant: "Know you not I must be about My Father's business?" (KJV). After *bar mitzvah,* He was to become Joseph's apprentice, to begin to be about his business of carpentry. Jesus gently reminded them that He was apprentice to His true Father's business. He announced Himself as His Father's disciple, submitted to Him. And the first act of the Father's disciple was to submit Himself to Joseph. This was the key to His authority: He could speak the words of the Father, *because* He was submitted to Him.

A Roman centurion recognized the authority contained in submission to higher power. This submission to authority is recognizable to those who are themselves submitted, and all are magnetically drawn to it. The centurion said, "For I, too, am a man under authority, with soldiers under me; and I say to this one, 'Go!' and he goes, and to another, 'Come!' and he comes, and to my slave, 'Do this!' and he does it" (Matt. 8:9).

He paralleled his relationship to Caesar, to the relationship that Jesus had to His Father. As the centurion submitted to Caesar, so he had authority over his troops with all the authority of Caesar behind him. If, however, he rebelled

146

against Caesar, so his troops would be free to rebel against him. Jesus said that this understanding of submission was great faith. When we are submitted to God all His power is behind us to accomplish His will, and out of that comes faith.

Because of this authority, given to Jesus by the Father, He never had to demand a title and was not upset when He didn't receive one. He did not push for superior seats at feasts. He didn't need that to prove His position. On the contrary, He, the greatest of all, took the position of the most menial servant, washing the disciples' feet. He did not need to be served in order to have their respect and obedience.

I began to realize that if I was to have authority it would be by being in submission to the elders of the church in Brooklyn. This was a heavy truth to swallow, for I had always approached an elders' meeting as if I was entering a war zone, looking upon them as intruders into my ministry. To begin to look at them as helpers of my faith, and fellow-workers in the ministry, to think of them as the other parts of the ministry in Salem was a major revolution in my heart. It was a gradual process that began deep within me in the area of attitudes and began to be worked out in my elders' meetings. At the same time I was also beginning to be aware that, as I was learning to submit in Brooklyn, so I knew authority and power in the New Jersey meetings, and among those who were being discipled.

All this took place over the period of many months since I had begun to accept the responsibility of discipling others. Then I faced the greatest test of this understanding. The burden of the school and the meetings in New Jersey made it impossible to truly be pastor to the congregation in Brooklyn. I also knew where my authority and power increasingly

lay. It was in the school and the meetings in mid and northern Jersey. Yet I could not think of leaving Salem, for here
was the source of the authority and power in submission to
the elders and fellowship with the Body. I knew I had to
leave the church as lead pastor, but I knew I couldn't leave
the church, for I needed them more than they needed me.

Floyd and I discussed it in the coffee shop on 5th Avenue
and decided to go to the mountains to spend some time in
waiting on the Lord. We returned convinced that this was
the way that we should take. As I went to the elders' meeting
that night I felt some of the old feelings. I was pretty certain
that I had the will of God, and surely they would have to
understand. But then a stronger sense of faith rose and
conquered. This was to be the test of all I had come to see: if
this was the will of God, then they would know it, and would
send me to do that will with their blessing. That would be
the secret of power and authority as I went.

That fall Sunday evening of 1973 I quietly told them what
I knew I had to do and waited for their reaction.

Alf broke the silence with an emotion-charged voice, "We
know you have to go but we don't want you to. We love you.
But we realize you must fulfill your ministry. So we send
you, in the name of the Lord." One by one the others
agreed, and I sat in awe of God's confirmation. The idea of
my remaining in the church as a teaching elder was a new
idea that took much discussion. By the time we came to
present it to the church, the elders had agreed that I should
remain part of that Body, sent out to teach.

Our immediate need was a house. The most logical place
was in northern New Jersey where the main arteries in and
out of the city came together. As Jean and I moved out of
the city a sense of peace, power and authority seemed to fill
the car. There had been many abortive attempts to do what
we were now doing, but this time we were moving with a

word from God in our hearts and the blessing of the elders. That kind of authority, according to Jesus, was the fertile ground of great faith.

We needed great faith for we had no money to buy a house. We were facing another test of submission and authority. If we were going to New Jersey, sent out by the Spirit and the church, then we could actively expect all of our needs would be supplied.

We drove to Allendale, where Dick Van Houten had his real estate office. He, along with a group of Spirit-filled businessmen, sponsored all of my meetings in north Jersey. I had first heard of Dick back in 1972. I had been speaking in a teenage camp in Stokes Forest. One of the campers, Donna Saint, listened enthusiastically to all I had to say and we had long discussions after each meeting. Early in the week she said, "Do you know Dick Van Houten?" I had never heard of him. She looked at me strangely and said, "But you must know him! He's behind everything that happens in northern New Jersey."

I nodded, not overly impressed or too interested, but asked, "Whereabouts?"

"You know, Allendale and Ramsey, where he lives."

I nodded again. "Well, I'm afraid I've never heard of Ramsey or of your friend." I spoke firmly trying to bring the conversation to an end.

"I guess you will soon," she said matter of factly. "There is a great work that goes on in his living room—kids are saved, receive the Baptism, and are healed. It would be fabulous if you could come and speak to us. Hey! If Mr. Van Houten asked you, would you come?"

I got up and laughed, "Sure! But I doubt he has ever heard of me either!"

After the camp I was to join my family in Pennsylvania for vacation, and I drove back to the city on my way to change clothes. I had packed my cases and was on my way out, but decided I had enough time to stop for a cup of tea. As I waited for the water to boil, the phone rang. I let it ring. As far as that phone was concerned I was on vacation! I was not going to answer it, but it rang on, and I finally grudgingly took the receiver from its cradle.

"You don't know me," an unfamiliar voice said. "My name is Dick Van Houten. I've heard of your meetings in Hazlet, and I believe it's time you came and gave us some meetings in North Jersey."

I smiled into the phone, "Yes. As it happens, I *have* heard of you, and I don't believe I have any choice but to come for meetings."

After our initial meeting, Dick and his fellow businessmen sponsored meetings in Ridgewood, and then we settled down to a weekly schedule of meetings that moved from Ramsey to Wyckoff and finally to Washington Township.

This October, 1973, our car slipped into his parking lot. I turned off the engine, and we drank it all in—the calm of the sleepy little town, and the great trees around the office, so different from Brooklyn, I reached for Jean's hand and prayed for a word of wisdom and a word of knowledge. "And Lord," I concluded, "cut through all the red tape of looking for a house, and lead us directly to the house you have for us."

Inside, Dick warmly greeted us, and we explained all that had happened since we had last talked, as well as how we now wanted to buy a house, even though we had no money. Dick was a businessman, but he also understood the ways of God, and our financial situation did not bother him. He picked up his books to show us what he had. He flipped through the pages, book after book with a faraway look in his eyes. "None of these are for you," he finally murmured. "But don't worry; God has one for you." He pulled two leaves from the book. "We might as well have a look at these," he said, "to give you an idea of what is around."

We looked, but spent most of the time visiting with Dick, because the three of us knew that none of these was the house God had in mind for us. We came back to his office, and as we stood on the steps, he paused and nodded to himself. "I know the house. It's not on the market yet, but it's going to be. And it happens to be right opposite ours." His eyes lit up. "You know, I've got the key, and I could show it to you, right now."

I glanced at Jean and grinned. "Let's go."

But as we turned on to Forest Road, Jean leaned over and whispered to me, "This is too expensive for us." The house was white with a window that covered most of the front wall. It took its form from a large peaked roof that extended down to include the garage on the right. In front was an expanse of lawn that I estimated would take about half an hour to mow. By the time we had looked over the house and wandered through the back garden, I was inclined to agree with her. We loved every inch of it, but it did look too expensive.

I stood alone in the copse at the end of the garden. I loved the feel of dry leaves around my feet, the smell of bark and moss in the air. Across the lawn, the house was haloed by trees all in various shades of fall. I praised God for the house, thanking Him for however He was going to get us to actually live here. We had prayed for a word of wisdom and now we went home resting in God that somehow the money for the down payment would come. We had long ago given up making our prayers into suggestion boxes to Deity. *How* He achieved His will was none of our business.

We were sitting in our living room in Brooklyn the next

151

day, when we received a phone call from Dick, who had been investigating mortgage possibilities. "I mentioned to one of the brothers about you coming to live out here, and he said he wanted to give money to help buy a house." I could hardly believe it! As soon as I hung up, I went back to tell Jean. During the next four days we had three similar calls and our down payment was complete.

The church received the announcement in much the same way as the elders and agreed with them that we should be sent out from the congregation while remaining a part of it. It was a number of weeks later that Jean and I knelt on the platform in front of the congregation, and the elders laid hands on me, sending me to teach in the renewal that was sweeping the Church on the East Coast. During the years, hands had been laid on me on many occasions, but I realized that this time would be unique. Kneeling under their hands, I understood in my heart what it meant, that I was under their authority, and from that position of safety could exercise authority in the sphere the Spirit had chosen to work through me.

They were not laying on hands to impart an anointing or send me to start something. Representing the congregation, they were recognizing a ministry already given by the Spirit, and were acknowledging the place of the Spirit's appointment. They were sending me to give myself wholly to that. Whenever I stood to minister, I would do so in the authority of the Lord Jesus, the power of the Holy Spirit and the covering of the Body of Christ in Brooklyn.

It was early February, 1974, when we moved into our house in Allendale, and I began giving myself fully to the ministry of teaching and discipling.

XV

It had never occurred to me that anyone but the devil would view what I was doing with concern. When I received the letter from Jack, it left me speechless.

He was a pastor who was a distant friend and we had enjoyed good fellowship whenever we met. He had been arranging meetings for me in the mid-state town where he lived, and when I saw the return address on the envelope, I assumed it contained a letter wrapping up the final details of the forthcoming meetings. Instead it was a cancellation. It bluntly stated that his religious superiors had all but ordered him not to have the meetings with me because of my doctrinal emphasis.

I read on, "They prefer I do not engage you because of your emphasis on discipleship." That puzzled me. They were Pentecostal as I was. How could we have such differences in doctrine as to necessitate closing the services? I felt no bitterness just sorrow for my friend and his superiors. My mind was wordless and numb.

Two days later, I sat opposite Jack in a diner halfway

between our homes. Jack avoided my eyes, as he sipped his coffee nervously. I didn't look forward to what would come next either, but knew we had to talk. I began, "Look Jack, you know me, I am open to correction. Go ahead, I'm ready to listen. If you believe I am preaching heresy, accuse me with witnesses before my elders and let them discipline me."

He looked up at me then and said slowly, "Malcolm, they just don't like the extreme position you are taking, especially in discipleship. And quite frankly, I don't either." His voice ended in a tired sigh.

"Can you give me some specifics?"

"Oh, come on, Malcolm, you must know what I am talking about." His face became red. "You're down there in Brooklyn, setting yourself up as some kind of —of—*guru*, a master with disciples around your feet. That's not far short of dictatorship, ordering them around and telling them how to run their lives." He warmed to his subject, leaning across the table, "That's not all: you take people away from the church, into home groups, making them into some kind of spiritual elite who are too good for regular churches. You are splitting the church right down the middle, and it's about time you realized it!"

People from surrounding booths began to turn in our direction, and he stopped with embarrassment. Picking up his coffee he looked at me over the cup. "Isn't that so?" he threw the words across the table in a hoarse stage whisper.

I could have wept for my brother. "Where did you hear all of this, Jack?" I asked wearily. He mentioned the names of two men. I knew them well, and I also knew that they had never been to our church, Bible school, or any of my meetings.

"Jack, shouldn't you or your people have asked *me* rather than take it on hearsay and rumor? Everything you have said is a distortion of the facts." And we plunged into a conversation that I would repeat to pastors and leaders many times over in the months ahead.

Discipleship is not a new word, or an invention added to the church in the last few years. The concept appears frequently in the pages of the New Testament. Matthew 28 describes the Church as a discipling community. Discipling *belongs* in the Church.

A new convert has a very real experience, based on a very small amount of truth. He has an immediate need of being taught who he is in Christ, and who Christ is in him. He is still blinking, unaccustomed to the light he has walked into. He is confused, looking for answers. At the same time, his spirit is unquestionably reborn, alive, new, filled with joy. His heart knows more than his head understands.

At that moment he needs to be apprenticed to the new life by a pastor who will tell him what has happened to him, who he is and where he is going. He needs to be shown by example how this miracle life works.

For years the Church has failed to do that one thing that Jesus commanded. Tragically, it has followed Hollywood more than Jesus, in putting pressure on the weakest spot in the baby Christian: the area of pride. If he has had any sensational or celebrity background of sin from which he has been dramatically rescued, he is placed before an eager public who want to hear the details of a sinful life more than of the miracle of grace that saved him. A new convert soon falls into pride, but not before he has become an authority on Christian living to thousands of people. A baby rules over the people.

But the average new unexploitable convert is just as pitiful. This one, who has no background that might lead him to stardom, falls into a pathetic round of meetings week after week that are characterized by songs about salvation, and sermons on how to be saved. It isn't long before he becomes bored with the repetition, and his Christianity settles down to a Sunday morning affair.

His kind of Christianity has no idea how to relate the Lordship of Christ to anything beyond the service on Sunday morning. He doesn't know how to bring his family life into line with the New Testament. His relationships in the home, at work, and with other church members are largely unaffected by the light of Christ. His only claim to being different is that he goes to church an hour a week.

This empty life cries out for more, as hunger cries for food. He wistfully knows that the ragged tempers, the seething envies and jealousies ought not to be, if Jesus is Lord. So there begins a sad pilgrimage from meeting to meeting, to anyone who promises to pray the prayer that will bring joy. They swing from having their problems cast out of them to seeking an experience of being overwhelmed by the power of God, always hoping that this time the cry will be satisfied. After a while the frustration is only deeper as the instant solutions are found wanting.

When the early Church spoke of a believer, or an adherent to the church, he *was* a disciple, taught in the faith and instructed in how to live it by those who were more mature in the Lord. This is not a hobby for the spiritual elite; this *is* the Church! It is the training of the babes in the truth that they have come into, the teaching of them in cooperation with the Spirit of Truth who is within them, and never being satisfied until they are complete in Christ. "And we proclaim Him, admonishing every man and teaching every man with all wisdom, that we may present every man complete in Christ" (Col. 1:28).

The truth that is in Jesus Christ is total truth. There is not an area of knowledge, or life, that does not need adjustment to it. The new babe must know exactly what Christ did when He died and rose again; *there* is the focal point of the ages and the source of all his Christian experience. He must understand what it is to walk in harmony with the Spirit, and his mind must be renewed to adjust to a life lived under the very real Lordship of Jesus. He will be introduced to a real world of the demonic, and he must learn how to stand triumphant, able to cope with attack and temptation. None of this is picked up by accident; it must be taught. If a church is doing its job, it is teaching this to each new believer.

But the very nature of such teaching demands that he has someone to show him *how*, someone to gently point out where the teaching should be applied in his life, under the guidance of the Holy Spirit. The Christian life is never viewed as a kind of smorgasbord where we take what we like and leave the rest. Its first words are a *command* to repent and believe the Gospel, and the epistles are filled with commands Paul gives to his spiritual children calling on them specifically to change their life style to fit in with what Christ has done for them, and who He is within them.

The fundamentalist end of the Church has applied pressure to change in regard to the dress code, hairstyle, and areas of entertainment while leaving many areas of personal relationships without discipline. It has left the Church filled with folk dressed the same but unable to love each other.

To disciple as we had come to understand from Scripture, would only build a church, never destroy it. Any pastor would admit that if every member of his church knew who they were in Christ and lived it, there would be a universal revolution, and the world would know that Christ is alive in any given community, in His Body.

This is all that the concept of discipleship is saying, as it calls pastors and leaders to take their people on from salvation to serious training in the truth, so that they may be able to train others who would in turn be able to train still others. It should never be limited to a Bible school or thought of as being only for the elite. This *is* the Church.

Jack had calmed down and was listening intently. He nodded slowly, "What you are saying sounds incredible, too good to be true, in fact. But I will admit you have the New Testament on your side. I spend my whole time as a pastor, trying to convince my people that it is worth remaining as a Christian, so we can reach heaven. But there's got to be a better way." His voice was husky as he spoke, and tears filled his eyes.

"Jack, if they knew who they were *now,* you couldn't stop them sharing and growing in grace." He didn't answer me but looked at me for a long time struggling to collect himself. Then he said, "Does this work in your church, or do they have to come to Bible school?"

"It's beginning to work in the church but we're not perfect yet! But we know where we are going. I wonder if some will ever learn, but it's spreading from the school through the congregation. In fact, some that Ray discipled now have little groups of their own."

I could see that he was torn now. His heart was being pulled in one direction, his intellect in another. He went to the attack one last time: "But aren't you really just making lots of little Malcolm Smiths, just followers of you?"

I had heard that accusation so many times that I smiled. "Certainly to begin with, their working out of their salvation is modeled after the way I work it out, but we are teaching them who *they* are. We are not teaching them dependence on us. We are teaching them dependence on Christ. After a while any dependence they might have originally had on the human falls away, and they stand tall in God. They will always have respect and a listening ear to what we say, but they are teaching others, and what we are enjoying then is very rich fellowship."

We finished our coffee in silence. Finally, Jack reached out his hand and took mine. "Forgive me for listening to hearsay, and not asking you directly," he said. "I understand where you are. If ever you come to my area, I'll be at your meetings, but I'm afraid I can't sponsor—you understand, don't you?"

I couldn't smile. I felt like weeping for a brother trapped in the system of religious dictatorship. "I understand, Jack, only too well."

XVI

I stepped on the gas, as I came on to Route 17 South, to get ahead of the truck that was fast closing behind. It was still dark, and there was no sign of dawn. I glanced at the clock, glowing green on the dashboard: 6:15 A.M. I was right on schedule this morning. I settled back into my seat for the hour drive ahead of me into Brooklyn.

The wheels of my car hissed on the wet pavement, as Waldwick and Hohokus fell behind me. It was cold, but not enough to freeze the moisture left from last night's rain. It was Tuesday and I enjoyed Tuesdays more than any other day, not only because I was teaching first-year theology, but also because I was always confronted by what we were doing. Ray lectured second-year on Tuesdays, and I knew that right now he was heading north on the Garden State Parkway. I praised God. If the school had accomplished nothing else, Ray was living proof of the results of discipling.

I remembered the day nearly nine months before, when after his three years of discipleship, we had ordained him and sent him to pastor a group of folk newly into the grace of God in Colts Neck, New Jersey. On a sultry day in June, I had sat beside him on the platform with the elders and had later solemnly laid hands on him, setting him apart for the ministry.

I chuckled, still feeling the ridiculousness of what we were doing by all that this world understands of ordination. A young man a few years old in Christ, with no seminary training or degree in theology, but was being set aside to minister the Word. His qualifications were that he had been trained in the Scriptures and apprenticed to Floyd and myself for three years. That morning I had scanned the congregation and seen families that had been led to Christ and discipled by Ray who were now discipling their own groups. There was a great ministry ahead for this brother, I remembered saying then, and certainly time had proven that. But how could we ever explain what we were doing?

What is the qualification for ministry? Seminary training, and degrees? However valuable they were, and we had nothing against them, I could not help but think of the many who, in spite of their degrees, had nothing to share with their congregations. Only God can qualify a man to minister, by giving him a ministry gift through His resurrected Son. When He has given, it can be nurtured and developed, but unless God has given, no amount of education will give it.

What training does a minister need? We are ministers of the new covenant, revealed in Jesus Christ and contained in the Scriptures We had immersed Ray in that for nearly three years, showing him how the eternal plan of God, the Good News to man, is revealed in Jesus Christ. He had timorously begun to share that and watched its dynamic results in others.

161

He had had problems after he had come through the first fears. One problem was, he liked to preach too much. He knew that one day he would be ministering full-time, and pulled at the bit to be away and doing just that.

He drove his cab in New York City during the evenings and into the night to provide for his family while he went to school. On the seat beside him was his Bible and notes, which he studied between fares. Stuck in traffic jams, sweating in the canyons of Manhattan, and driving through garbage-strewn streets of Brownsville, he had lived for the day when he would be free to just preach.

The Spirit began to show him that it was his relationship to God that counted far more than preaching. His discontent at that time indicated that he was in love with preaching more than God Himself. Faced with this, he had made a hard but very deliberate choice to accept life as it was *now,* and to worship God, rather than live in a non-existent future and be angry at the way things were. He accepted his cab from God, and the fares as God's gift, and rejoiced in God until He should change his situation.

As graduation of that first group of students had approached, the elders had discussed where each might fit in the church. With Ray, we knew that he would soon be ministering as a pastor, and we discussed his readiness. Our biggest fear was that he was so young in the Lord. Would he fall through pride? Did he really understand his reliance on the rest of the Body, or was he thinking of himself as a lone crusader out to change the world?

Before we had a chance to ask him, he came to us and asked if we would consider ordaining him. The door had now opened up for his ministry to support him full-time, but he did not want to go without the local Body recognizing and sending him.

At the elders meeting where we talked with him, it was Joseph Olsen who asked him, "What would you do if we refused to ordain you at this time?"

Ray didn't hesitate, "I would remain as I am until you felt I was ready. I cannot minister without the Body behind me. I had already decided that I wouldn't move, unless the elders felt I was ready." That simple honest answer convinced us that he was in no danger of pride while in dependence on the Body, and after prayer we decided to ordain him.

So it was on that hot day in June, with the wail of distant emergency vehicles coming through the open windows, that Ray was ordained. Floyd had explained that we were not about to make Ray a minister, but rather recognize that God had already made him one, and now was sending him out to minister in the Body of Christ. He had proved himself before the congregation and elders, we were only acknowledging what God had already accomplished.

Ray and his wife had knelt as we laid hands on him, and set him aside to the ministry. Memories had surged through Floyd and myself, as we remembered the three years we had spent with this young man, from the day he had walked in and sat at the back, a hippie cab driver. Ray began to weep, remembering the years of God's dealings before he knew who God was.

Someone began to sing *Amazing Grace,* and they were never more in the Spirit than at that moment. Now, recalling, I hummed it softly in the car, as I traveled down Route 17.

In addition to his pastoral duties in Colts Neck, Ray was also lecturing each Tuesday in the school. It would be good to see him and hear what was happening in the new work.

Joanne would be there today to pick up some lectures

before taking some first-year girls with her to minister in women's Bible studies in New Jersey. She had a number of such groups, almost more than she could keep up with, as well as children's meetings throughout the area. I smiled as I remembered her complaint the previous week. She had taken me aside, "The girls in first-year are coming to me with their problems, and it's a responsibility I'm scared of." I laughed loud and long. "Remember, Jo, when I said that to you! Just share with them what I have shared with you. They came to me, and I sent them to you."

A red and yellow sign beckoned up ahead through the darkness, and I began pulling the car over. Within minutes I was sipping coffee in the Paramus Diner, going over the notes for the morning lectures. The subject thrilled me, the awesome discovery of who God was.

By the time Route 17 passed through Rutherford, dawn was breaking in the east. New York City spread out in front of me etched black against the golden red glory of the dawn. Rockefeller Center, the Empire State Building and the World Trade Center stood stark against the crimson sky. The view was only visible in the moments of turning off Route 17 to Route 3, and I drank in every second of it, not only praising God for its beauty but to feel the ache for the city that would not let me go.

Half an hour later, I was coming over the Verrazano Bridge, the sun blinding me, Brooklyn and Queens a checkerboard of streets and houses as far as the eye could see.

At the coffee-break that morning, I moved among the students—nearly fifty of them—visiting, and sharing, answering a question here and there. It was a long way from three and a half years ago when ten of us sat around the coffee pot. Ray came down from lecturing the second-year students, and we warmly embraced. He was excited at the prospect of bringing in fourteen of his disciples to baptize them the following Sunday.

A group had gathered by the bulletin board to read an unusually early announcement of a summer seminar to be held in Landisville, Pennsylvania. I was one of the speakers, and although I already knew who the other speaker was, the sight of the little green-and-white folder blinded my eyes with tears of joy. The photographs of the two featured speakers were side by side on the front page, myself and Ray. We were Bible teachers together in the same Bible conference.

Joanne had joined us and was reading the announcement over my shoulder. "That is an historic document," she said softly. I nodded slowly. It was on this very spot four years before, a newborn babe in Christ had joined himself to us to be discipled. Now we stood side by side ministering in the Gospel.

Was it possible to take a hippie and teach, show, and mature him in cooperation with the Holy Spirit? Yes, at that moment I was never more convinced of God's method.

The bell rang. I walked away from the students who began to move to their various sharing groups. I had a meeting with Floyd, and had to leave. As I turned for a last look at the scurrying students, Peter waved as he went into the kitchen, and Joyce followed him with the others who met there. There was Ann, Doug, Ed, Mike, Tim, each one another Ray, another Joanne, each of them already well on their way to ministry.

But that's another story.

EPILOG

A year has slipped by. The school has become larger. Many students commute each day, as I do, from New Jersey. Increasingly, a percentage of the school has had nothing to do with the actual functioning of the local church out of which it was born. For myself, I was involved more and more in the area in which I lived, becoming an institutional president of the school. I was lecturing on its premises, but having no fellowship with it.

Although dimly aware of this, it was only as I pored over old journals and notes, piecing together the story of the vision of that New Year's morning, that I realized how far we had come. I knew that in another five years we would have moved so far that we would be unrecognizable as the group of disciples I was writing about.

Other changes were taking place. A fellowship had been formed in Bergen County where I lived that met each Sunday morning to work out the principles of New Testament fellowship and commitment. As the chapters of the book were written and re-written, I knew that I had to return to the original command the Spirit had given me: to train men and women in the context of the fellowship where I lived so that the teaching could be observed and lived out on a practical level. It also was apparent that we could only minister to a few at a time.

In January, 1976, I tendered my resignation as president of the school in Brooklyn. There was no break in fellowship, and the school there will continue fulfilling a need in the Body of Christ. In the fall we shall begin training men and women in Bergen County in the context of the fellowship of believers there. It will be a full-time school, lasting for five months, and limited to twenty students at a time, enabling me to give myself wholly to them.

I sit in my Allendale, New Jersey, office and write this last paragraph with a smile. God has a sense of humor. In writing to tell *others* of what we were doing, the Holy Spirit has gently brought *me* back on course to make sure I keep on doing it.